Via

Hiking the White Trail
in Bosnia & Herzegovina

The Bradt Trekking Guide

Tim Clancy

www.bradtguides.com

Bradt Travel Guides Ltd, UK
The Globe Pequot Press Inc, USA

edition
1

First published January 2018
Bradt Travel Guides Ltd
IDC House, The Vale, Chalfont St Peter, Bucks SL9 9RZ, England
www.bradtguides.com
Print edition published in the USA by The Globe Pequot Press Inc,
PO Box 480, Guilford, Connecticut 06437-0480

Via Dinarica is the project jointly funded by USAID and the UNDP in Bosnia and
Herzegovina. The contents of this publication do not necessarily reflect the views of USAID,
nor the UNDP.

ISBN: 978 1 78477 051 8 (print)
e-ISBN: 978 1 78477 535 3 (e-pub)
e-ISBN: 978 1 78477 436 3 (mobi)

British Library Cataloguing in Publication Data
A catalogue record for this book is available from the British Library

Photographs
Adnan Bubalo (AB); Dreamstime.com: Slavenko Vukasović (SV/D); Esmera Kanalstein (EK);
Olja Latinović (OL); Kenan Muftić (KM); Elma Okić (EO); Shutterstock.com: balkanyrudej
(b/S), Bosnian (B/S), Lucertolone (L/S), mapraest (m/S); Miro Šumanović (MS)

Front cover Hiker (AB)
Back cover Looking across the Tisovica Valley to Prenj (AB)
Title page Via Dinarica signage (OL); view of Trnovačko Lake from Maglić (AB); Umoljani
mosque (AB)
Page 1 Hikers on Bregoč Peak (KM); *page 67* View of Prenj from Čvrsnica Mountain (OL)

Maps Outdooractive Kartografie; David McCutcheon FBCart.S

Typeset by Ian Spick, Bradt Travel Guides Ltd
Production managed by Jellyfish Print Solutions; printed in the United Kingdom
Digital conversion by www.dataworks.co.in

ABOUT THIS GUIDE

MAPS This book has been designed so you can walk the Via Dinarica using the maps included. The route of the Via Dinarica has been walked, as have some, though not all, of the paths leading off it.

Scale The maps are at a scale of 1:45,000 (2.2cm represents 1km).

Orientation All the maps in this guide are oriented page north, that is N is the top of the page as you read it.

Symbols A key to the symbols used on the maps is on page vii.

Accommodation In order to keep the maps uncluttered and easy to use, only those accommodation and restaurant options that occur along, or conveniently close to, the route are shown. Not all places shown on the maps are included in the text.

HEIGHTS AND DISTANCES Throughout this book, elevations are given in metres (m) and distances in kilometres (km).

TIMINGS The timing given in the introduction to each stage refers to an average walking speed, and does not include breaks or stopping time (as a general rule of thumb, add 10 minutes to every hour, plus time to stop for lunch).

GRADING Each stage is graded easy/moderate/difficult. A short summary of the terrain and any particular difficulties encountered is given in the introduction to each stage. A profile chart shows elevation and distance.

TRUE RIGHT/LEFT All references to which side (bank) of a river you're on are given as true right/left, that is they refer to the right/left bank as seen when facing downstream.

LANDLINE AND MOBILE NUMBERS Landlines in Bosnia and Herzegovina (BiH) comprise a nine-digit number beginning with 03 or 05. Mobile-phone numbers are also nine digits, but begin 06. The international code for Bosnia and Herzegovina is +387. When calling from outside BiH, the zero (from the area code of the region calling) is dropped. The zero is retained for in-country calls.

PRICES The currency in BiH is KM (BAM), although euros are accepted in some places. The KM is fixed to the euro (1 = 1.95KM).

Acknowledgements

Authors: Tim Clancy, Kenan Muftić, Maggie Cormack
Contributing Authors: Džana Bordanić, Jim Marshall, Esmera Kanalstein, Eva Smeele, Matthieu Couedel, Rudolf Abraham
Via Dinarica Photographers: Adnan Bubalo, Olja Latinović, Elma Okić, Tihomir Crnjać, Kenan Muftić, Miro Šumanović

There are quite a lot of people to acknowledge, not just for their contributions to this hiking guide to the Via Dinarica White Trail in Bosnia and Herzegovina but also for making the Via Dinarica a reality.

The Sarajevo-based NGO Terra Dinarica has done a great deal of the heavy lifting in making the Via Dinarica a reality. Led by Kenan Muftić and Olja Latinović, these two covered the entire country top to bottom, worked with local actors, walked trails, fixed trails, marked trails, and did pretty much everything under the sun to make this happen. Džana Bordanić and Amra Muftić were their steadfast support. The UNDP Via Dinarica Project team was key in implementing all this: Božena Kaltak, Mirna Kajgana, and Marina Škobić worked tirelessly in keeping things on track. As members of the Via Dinarica Project Board, BiH Ministry of Foreign Trade and Economic Relations, the Ministry of Environment and Tourism of the Federation of Bosnia and Herzegovina, and the Ministry of Trade and Tourism of Republika Srpska recognized the value of the Project and continuously provide support to its implementation. Special thanks go to the USAID Mission to BiH as a major Project funder.

A lot of the credit, however, must go to the ordinary people who live along, and with, the Via Dinarica every day. This is their home. They are the keepers of this precious mountain range and without their lifelong commitment to the protection and sustainable utilisation of this mountain gem, none of this would be possible. The list is long but the credit is well deserved:

PD Željezničar, Sarajevo; PSD Lelija, Kalinovik; NVO Cetina Prenj, Jablanica; PD Orlova stina, Tomislavgrad; GSS Konjic, Konjic; HPD Pločno, Posušje; PD Visočica, Sarajevo; PD 'Prenj-Glogošnica 1979', Jablanica; PSD 'Vilinac', Jablanica; Sutjeska National Park; Blidinje Nature Park; Visit Konjic; Halit Levent Sirin and Turkish Airlines; Lasta Travel; Braco Babić, Miro Šumanović, Mehmed Prelić, Dejan Pavlović, Željko Lalović, Novak Govedarica, Dušan Lalović, Ante Vukadin, Marjan Džikić, Edin Širić, Aldin Širić, Ajdin Zebić, Zlatko Papac, Maggie Cormack, Hana Čurak; Via Dinarica Croatia team: Gordan Papac, Nedo Pinezić, Alan Čaplar, Dorijan Klasnić, Valetina Futač, Marija Jurčević, and all other project partners, beneficiaries, stakeholders and friends of Via Dinarica.

Contents

PART TWO – WHITE TRAIL STAGES IN BOSNIA AND HERZEGOVINA **67**

UPDATES WEBSITE

You can post your comments and recommendations, and read feedback and updates from other readers online at **w** bradtupdates. com/viadinarica.

Featured sites on the Via Dinarica

	Archaeological site		Motel
	Café		Mountain hut
	Camping		Mountain inn
	Canyon		Mountain lodge
	Cave		Museum
	Cemetery		National Park/Nature Park
	Church/chapel		Other point of interest
	Equestrian centre with accommodation		Pansion
	Farm with accommodation		Parking
	Food/bakery		Petrol station
	Forest		Pizzeria
	Geological site		Private hut
	Guesthouse/household		Private room
	Historic site		Restaurant
	Hospital/health centre		Shelter
	Hotel		Spring
	Information centre		Start/finish
	Lake		Stream
	Mill		Summit (height in metres)
	Monastery		Viewpoint
	Monument		Wayside cross
	Mosque		Wayside shrine

Other sites

€	Bank		Mosque
	Bus stop		Parking
	Cemetery		Petrol station
	Church, chapel		Railway station
	Cinema		Restaurant
	Electricity station	1015	Summit (height in metres)
	Hospital		Viewpoint
	Monument		Windfarm

FEEDBACK REQUEST AND UPDATES WEBSITE

At Bradt Travel Guides we're aware that guidebooks start to go out of date on the day they're published – and that you, our readers, are out there in the field doing research of your own. You'll find out before us when a fine new family-run hotel opens or a favourite restaurant changes hands and goes downhill. So why not write and tell us about your experiences? Contact us on ☎01753 893444 or e info@bradtguides.com. We will forward emails to the author who may post updates on the Bradt website at e bradtupdates.com/viadinarica. Alternatively you can add a review of the book to w bradtguides.com or Amazon.

*This designation is without prejudice to positions on status, and is in line with UNSCR 1244/1999 and the ICJ Opinion on the Kosovo declaration of independence.

viii

Introducing the Via Dinarica
... more than just a trail

The Via Dinarica is the world's newest long-distance trail that extends the entire length of the Dinaric Alps from Slovenia to Albania and Kosovo*. There are three trails – the White, Green and Blue – all linked by world-class hiking, biking and rafting routes, offering a multitude of adventure flavours for adrenaline seekers and nature lovers alike. While the Green and Blue Trails are still under development, the main White Trail follows the natural flow of the highest spine of the Dinaric Alps as it weaves through a large part of the western Balkans. This is the main trail along the entire length of the Via Dinarica. The White Trail includes all of the highest peaks in each respective country. Although there is a plethora of activities along this main trail, such as mountain biking and rafting, its main function is as a hiking trail. The White Trail is clearly defined and operational, with Bosnia and Herzegovina (BiH) being one of the few countries to have the entire route marked with Via Dinarica signage. But the Via Dinarica is so much more than a trail. It's also about the people and their places that make it so special.

The concept of the Via Dinarica was born when a Croatian hiking enthusiast named Gordan Papac decided to start uploading trip descriptions, maps and photos of his adventures throughout the Dinaric Alps to **w** summitpost.org. For years he had trekked this little-known mountain chain and became the go-to source for information on what he coined to be the Via Dinarica.

The idea didn't gain much momentum other than posting hikes on **w** summitpost.org until other hiking enthusiasts, ecotourism companies and even international donors began toying with the idea of taking the Via Dinarica from an idea to reality. A few small projects and many meetings later, the UN/UNDP Resident Coordinator/Representative in BiH, Yuri Afansiev, heeded the calls to fund a pilot project to hike the entire trail from Albania to Slovenia. He courted his counterpart, David Barth, USAID BiH Mission Director, who readily agreed. In summer 2013, the first full-length exploratory hike of the Via Dinarica was in motion. The UNDP- and USAID-funded first Via Dinarica expedition was conceptualised by Tim Clancy, led by Kenan Muftić, and filmed by local photographer Elma Okić. They hiked for three months, talking to local people, mapping the resources and trail conditions, and entering

GPS coordinates. What they found confirmed what we all believed – that the Via Dinarica is a world-class hiking destination.

That pilot was followed by a larger, three-year project funded by the same donors and implemented by the UNDP and its field partner Terra Dinarica, a local NGO based in Sarajevo dedicated to the development, protection and promotion of the Dinaric Alps and the Via Dinarica. This is when many local mountain associations and individuals stepped up to create what is today the 350km of the Via Dinarica White Trail in Bosnia and Herzegovina. This is truly a community-based, grass-roots movement to protect and sustainably develop their highland home and as such has been recognised and continuously supported by Peter Duffy, current USAID BiH Mission Director, and Sezin Sinanoglu, current UN/UNDP BiH Resident Coordinator/Representative.

On the Via Dinarica, the natural meets culture in enchanting ways. The still-thriving highland communities prove that no matter how remote you go, you're never terribly far from an adventure or a hot and hearty meal with a friendly local. Invading armies may have failed to conquer these mountains over the region's sometime turbulent past, but the Via Dinarica will lead you along footpaths that take you right to the heart of their magic, aided by the expertise and hospitality of the still-thriving highland communities. One of the most remarkable traits of the Via Dinarica, which sets it apart from other long-distance trails, is that it offers a rare glimpse into ancient cultures that have survived the manifold tests of time.

SEND US YOUR SNAPS!

We'd love to follow your adventures using our *Via Dinarica* guide – why not send us your photos and stories via Twitter (@BradtGuides) and Instagram (@bradtguides) using the hashtag #viadinarica. Alternatively, you can upload your photos directly to the gallery on the Via Dinarica destination page via our website (*www.bradtguides.com/viadinarica*).

Part One

GENERAL INFORMATION

*This designation is without prejudice to positions on status, and is in line with UNSCR 1244/1999 and the
ICJ Opinion on the Kosovo declaration of independence.

1
Background Information

GEOGRAPHY

The Dinaric Alps are rugged mountains composed of limestone and dolomite, with high karstic plateaus from which rocky peaks jut into the skies, and powerful rivers flow through deep gorges. The vegetation ranges from Mediterranean to European continental and Alpine, as the mountains form the barrier between the Adriatic Sea and continental central and eastern Europe. Their fauna includes carnivores such as bears, wolves, lynxes and other wild cats, as well as grazing livestock such as sheep and goats. Summits offer views on to moon-like karst landscapes and grassy, undulating hills, forested river valleys and occasionally the azure-blue Adriatic Sea. The contrasts are striking.

Named after the glorious **Dinara Mountain** that spans the border between Croatia and Bosnia and Herzegovina, the **Dinaric Alps** are a mountain chain that connect many different European ranges. They extend from the southern edges of the **European Alps** in Slovenia and Italy toward the western end of the **Balkan Peninsula**, northeast of the **Adriatic Sea** and south of the **Sava river basin** in the **Hungarian (Pannonian) Plain**. They touch the westernmost parts of the old **Rhodope Mountains** in central and southern Serbia, and reach the **Pindus Mountain** chain in northern Albania and the **Šara Mountains** near Kosovo* on their southeast end. The area that is scientifically known as the *Dinarides* refers to a tectonic unit shared by the Julian Alps in Slovenia and Italy and the Šara–Pindus system in Albania, Macedonia and Greece. This unit is larger than the area known as the **Dinaric Alps**. The Dinaric Alps mountain system is around 650–700km (c450 miles) long and between 50km and 200km wide, and it widens as it stretches southeast. It consists of more than 200 mountains, shared among eight nations: Slovenia, Italy, Croatia, Bosnia and Herzegovina, Montenegro, Serbia, Kosovo* and Albania.

Almost all **eastern Adriatic islands** along the coasts of Croatia and Montenegro belong to this mountain system. They are the former foothills of the Dinaric Alps, which became partially submerged by seawater in earlier geological history. The predominant **northwest–**

southeast direction (the so-called Dinaric direction) of the Dinaric Alps is one of its distinct characteristics. The mountains are defined and shaped by karstic valleys, fields and river flows that generally follow this Dinaric direction. They abound in a **variety of relief formations** that result from **erosive-denudation processes** (the destructive work of water, wind, ice) that strongly impact their mainly limestone faces. They are also diverse in appearance, geomorphology, climate, and natural, cultural and sociological background. Parts of the Dinaric Alps are the most rugged, remote and pristine natural areas in Europe, and their great diversity makes visiting them a truly unique experience.

MOUNTAINS The European Alps have been divided into groups and subgroups that are based on their geomorphological characteristics, as well as the historical traditions that designated them apart. However, the Dinaric Alps are more diverse, and have been harder to define, than the western European Alps. The Dinaric Alps abound in a great variety of terrain, geological structures and biodiversity. Little is scientifically known about many parts of this wild mountain chain, and the history of this region is so wrought with complex political divisions that it has always been contentious to define or name anything. In the end, the main, recognised division of the Dinaric Alps is three belts, or zones, that run parallel from northwest to southeast, through the length of the chain. These are the Maritime, or Southwestern Belt, the Central Belt and the Northeastern Belt. Certain mountain groups, or clusters, are also specifically distinguished, such as Prokletije, Durmitor and Velebit.

Mountain divisions The **Maritime Belt,** or **Southeastern Belt**, is made up of the first row of Dinaric Alps, which border the Adriatic Sea. They are mainly characterised by limestone, from the Cretaceous period, and flysch soils from the Eocene period. There are four main regions of this belt: the northern Adriatic, especially Istria and the islands that formerly represented the foothills of the Alps; the Dalmatia region, which includes the Dalmatian coast with its many islands as well as Mediterranean Herzegovina; the region of Maritime and central Montenegro including the karstic Katunska Plateau and the Rudine area; and the mountains of Lower Herzegovina.

The **Central Belt,** or **High Dinaric Alps**, is the largest belt and encompasses most of the mountain regions. It is mainly built of limestone from the Mesozoic period. Included are the mountains of the high karstic plateaus of Slovenia and Croatia, such as the Gorski kotar Plateau and all of Snežnik, as well as the Velika Kapela group; the Lika region of Croatia, which houses Velebit; the Dinara massif and the Cincar group and Raduša mountain range; the mountains of high

▲ Views of Maglić from Zelengora Mountain in Sutjeska National Park (KM)

Herzegovina, including Čvrsnica, Prenj and Velež; the central Bosnian and Herzegovinian mountains such as Zelengora, Maglić and Volujak, Vranica and Bjelašnica; and the high mountains of Montenegro, especially the Prokletije range and Durmitor, the Sinjajevina massif, Komovi and Bjelasica.

The Northeastern Belt is more complex – it is where the Dinaric Alps meet the Pannonian/Hungarian plain, where millions of years ago was the Pannonian Sea. The mountains here hold layers of eruptive rocks from the Paleozoic period, and sediments of the Pannonian Sea. This area has less porous karst topography, with normal, above-ground water flows. This belt is characterised by low, green mountains with rolling hills. The mountain regions here include the Dolenjska region in Slovenia and the Croatian northwest; the mountains of central and eastern Bosnia, especially Vlašić and Jahorina; the mountains of Stari Vlah and Raška (Sandžak), including the Polimlje-Podrinje group and Zlatar-Pešter group; the mountains of northwestern Serbia; and the Peri-Pannonian or pre-Dinaric mountains.

RIVERS The rivers of the Dinaric Alps flow through karst region, offering abundant springs (*vrelo*), waterfalls (*slapovi*) and many canyon-like valleys. Three-quarters of them flow eastwards to the Black Sea, while the remaining 25% drain into the Adriatic. This includes the great **Danube River**; its largest tributary is the **Sava** which originates in the Slovenian Alps, and into which also flow the **Krka**, **Kupa**, **Una**, **Vrbas**, **Bosna** and **Drina** rivers.

The main rivers flowing into the Adriatic Sea are **Soča/Isonzo** (137km), **Krka (Dalmatian)** (71km), **Cetina** (106km), **Zrmanja** (69km), **Neretva** (213km), **Zeta** (65km), **Morača** (97km), **Bojana/Buna** and **Drim/Drin** (109km). The only river that cuts through the Maritime and Central Dinarics is the **Neretva**, providing a passage into the valley of the **Bosna River** by way of the Ivan sedlo Pass (967m). Despite the fact that most of the Dinaric rivers cut through limestone gorges, many of them, especially in the northern parts of the chain, have long been important traffic routes, because there were no easier options (no low-lying mountain passes) in the past. Other rivers have carved their canyons deeply through limestone rock, forging unapproachable barriers against any serious contacts and travel; these have acted as division-lines between family clans and warring regions. Because these rivers are rich in waterfalls, they are rich in Salmonidae (or salmonids) fish species. They are also used, controversially, for hydro-electric power plants.

Lakes There are more than 200 lakes throughout the Dinaric Alps. They vary in origin from karstic, tectonic, glacial, travertine, fluviokarstic, or fluvial; most of them are smaller than 10km².

- Karstic lakes formed by karstic erosion are, eg: **Red and Blue lakes** (Crveno and Modro jezero) near Imotski (Croatia, Dalmatia)

▼ Trnovačko Lake seen from Maglić in Sutjeska National Park (AB)

- Travertine lakes are formed by the accumulation of sediments of marl in riverbeds, such as **Pliva lake** (Plivsko jezero) and **Plitvice lakes** (Plitvička jezera).
- If erosion is combined with tectonic sinking, those lakes are known as karstic-tectonic, such as **Lake Shkodra** (Skadarsko jezero).
- A type of karstic lake includes periodically flooded areas of karstic fields, such as **Cerknica field** (Cerkniško polje), **Popovo field** (Popovo polje), **Livno field** (Livanjsko polje), **Kosinj field** (Kosinjsko polje) and others.
- Glacial lakes can be found in elevated areas of Montenegro and Bosnia and Herzegovina. They are mostly smaller, but they are beautiful and many people call them 'mountain eyes' (18 such lakes are on **Durmitor**, 6 on **Bjelasica**). There are also lakes of glacial origin situated at the foothills of high mountains, where the water dammed by sediments drifted here through the glaciers. Such lakes are **Plav lake** (Plavsko jezero) and **Biograd lake** (Biogradsko jezero).

GEOLOGY

Overall, the main Alpine chains of Europe resulted from the subduction of Tethyan oceanic crust followed by a continent collision between African and European lithospheric plates. The Alpine orogenesys was very complex and occurred in several phases from the middle Cretaceous to the Neogene, of which the collision between Europe and Africa was only one.

The Dinaric Alps lack ore minerals. The exemptions are the mountains of central and northern Bosnia and some other isolated regions, where some of the mountains do not consist of limestone alone, but of other or older rocks.

DINARIC KARST Out of all the natural characteristics of the Dinaric Alps mountain chain, the most important and the most known is **karst** (also known as **Dinaric karst**). Karst is a type of relief with formed hydrographic and geomorphological shapes and structures, created by water penetrating into soluble rocks such as dolomite, gypsum and especially **limestone**. Karstic action is very much present in Dinaric areas that are chiefly composed of limestone. Most of the rocks in the Dinaric Mountains are late Paleozoic and Mesozoic limestone and dolomite. The rest of the chain is characterised by clastic flysch-like sediments, occasionally interbedded with limestone layers. Limestone in this area comes from the **former Tethys sea** (placed here 200 million years ago) from which more vast plates raised later, including the Adriatic and Dinaric plates.

The Dinaric karst area accounts for more than half of the surface of all the Dinarics. This area comprises the southwestern half of the chain, stretching from the Italian/Slovenian border all the way to the Skadar/Scutari Basin in Montenegro and Albania. The Dinaric mountain regions, already difficult to access, are even more inhospitable thanks to this intensive karstic action. This natural characteristic is one of the main reasons for depopulation of this area and its economic decay, over decades and centuries.

In spite of high rainfall averages in many karstic areas in the Dinarics, the coastal side of the chain has few surface watercourses, because rainwater quickly sinks underground into the crevices and cavities in the limestone. As you move inland and to higher ground the rainfall levels are still high, supporting the forming of dense forest covers (in the Notranjska area of Slovenia, Gorski kotar area of Croatia, and northern parts of western Bosnia). Still further inland, limestone areas are less frequent. Locally, there are karstic areas even in central and southeastern parts of the chain, but they are home to other less-porous rocks (schists, greywackes, serpentines and crystalline rocks), which hold surface flows and huge expanses of forests and other vegetation. This kind of karst is called **covered**, or **green karst**, because karstic processes are still taking place under the surface mantle of vegetation and humus-soil.

Closer to the coast, **bare karst** predominates. Here the forests were felled many centuries ago to provide the large quantities of timber required by the coastal towns and villages for shipbuilding and domestic consumption. Some of the largest quantities of timber were taken to Venice, Italy for millions of wooded pylons that hold up the basements of buildings in this 'floating' city. After this deforestation, the unprotected topsoil was washed away and the bare white limestone exposed, leaving a barren but magnificent landscape of bare karst. These areas of bare karst are clearly seen from space as white regions (especially the island of Pag, the Dalmatian hinterland, lower Herzegovina and the Montenegrin hinterland), in contrast to other wooded areas of the Dinarics.

Karst got its **name** after the Kras region in Slovenia and Italy (Italian Carso), a desolate, stony and waterless region situated inland from Trieste. The processes of karst formation were first studied by geologists and geographers in this area and the adjective 'karstic' has become a general term applied to any area where such processes have been at work (eg: areas in Slovakia, China, the USA, etc). The word is of Indo-European origin (*kar* meaning 'stone').

Karst develops after dissolving limestone in water, which contains carbon dioxide (CO_2). This is generally a result of mildly acidic rainfall acting on soluble limestone. The rain picks up CO_2 (which dissolves in water) when passing through the atmosphere. This whole process is called **karstification**.

CLIMATE

The mountains of the Dinaric Alps are under the influence of **three climates**. A **Mediterranean climate** governs the narrow coastal belt and the islands of the Adriatic Sea, creating hot, dry summers and mild, rainy winters. The high coastal slopes are very hot and sunny during the summer. These form the boundary between the Mediterranean coast and the **Alpine climate** beyond; here, warm, humid sea air clashes with colder mountain air, resulting in some of the highest levels of precipitation in Europe. In certain areas such as Velebit in Croatia, this coastal mountain barrier rises to such heights that it completely blocks the maritime climate from entering further inland. In other places, such as the Neretva or Zeta river valleys, the Mediterranean air penetrates further inland all the way to the Central Dinaric Belt.

Most of the Dinaric Alps bear a classical **mountainous or Alpine climate**, with heavy rainfalls, short and cool summers and long, snowy winters. Cold air descends into mountain valleys and fields during the winter, but in the summer these low-lying areas warm up quickly. The coldest areas can get down to −40ºC during the winter. The northern and northeastern edge of the Dinaric Alps enjoy a mixture of Alpine and **European continental climates**, with warm summers and cold winters.

FLORA AND FAUNA   *Džana Bordanić*

The Dinaric region is characterised by a high level of biodiversity for many different reasons. The limestone-dolomite bedrock and the formation of various types of soil, diverse climatic conditions, and unique physical and geographical characteristics, have had a positive impact on the flora and fauna of this region.

Special types of habitat such as wetlands that form around mountain springs and streams, as well as peatland ecosystems (peat bogs), can be found at the peaks of the Dinarides. A peatland is a type of wetland that is underlain by peat in various stages of decay. These ecosystems are under

FORESTS

Bosnia and Herzegovina is blessed with many wonders of nature. Perhaps one of its greatest gifts is the marvellous forests that cover slightly less than half the country. Although there has been significant deforestation due to unregulated clear-cutting, the countryside and mountainsides are still home to thick forests of beech, oak, chestnut, spruce and literally dozens of other types of trees.

▲ The endemic Bosnian lily is found in many areas on the Via Dinarica (OL)

anthropogenic pressures, mainly due to climate change and the overexploitation of peat.

It is important to mention the ecosystems of alpine grassland, which cover large areas of the Via Dinarica White Trail. These are specific ecosystems in which extreme climatic conditions prevail. Low temperatures, strong winds and longer snow retention are responsible for a short period of growth for vegetation. Plants here have adapted to such conditions, as have their pollinators. A result of the struggle to survive and adapt is an occurrence called 'grandifolia' or the occurrence of very large flowers.

FLORA Some habitats are natural refuge areas for flora and vegetation, as the entire Dinaric Arc region was a refuge for species during the last glacial period. Many rivers of the Dinaric Alps have cut impressive canyons that separate the mountain ranges. Ecologically speaking, the most valuable gene pool is located in the deep and difficult-to-reach river canyons, where certain rare, endangered and endemic species reside. It is important to protect these species from negative anthropogenic impact, primarily from the construction of hydro-electric power plants that are built without environmental impact assessments being carried out.

Rare stenoendemic species have created habitats on the Prenj–Čvrsnica–Velež mountain complex and the Neretva canyon, as well as the canyons of its tributaries. This area is the largest centre of endemic species in Bosnia and Herzegovina, and is known as the 'Prenj endemic centre'.

FAUNA The diversity of fauna in this region could fill several books. The most essential to mention are the endangered large **mammals**, and the vital importance of refraining from hunting and poaching cannot be overstated. In particular, these mammals include the **brown bear** (*Ursus arctos*), **wolf** (*Canis lupus*), **lynx** (*Lynx lynx*) and **chamois** (*Rupicapra rupicapra*). The disappearance of these animals would have long-term consequences that would affect the food chain and essential ecosystem balance.

Fish and **game** are abundant in Bosnia and Herzegovina. Most of the freshwater rivers are teeming with trout; carp, eel and bass are found throughout the country.

The Dinaric cave systems are teeming with ecological diversity. Animal species that live in caves are adapted to very specific conditions, and they develop unique characteristics. Postojna in Slovenia and Vjetrenica in Bosnia and Herzegovina are particular biodiversity hotspots. However, it is important to note that many caves here have yet to be fully investigated and some have never been explored. These are real treasures, and have great potential for scientific advancement.

The Dinaric Alps are also valuable habitats for a diversity of **bird** species, and home to many specially protected areas and Ramsar sites (areas of international importance). Examples of Important Bird Areas in Albania are Prokletije, Thethi, Lake Shkodra and Velipoja. In Bosnia and Herzegovina Ramsar sites include Bardača Lake, Hutovo blato and Livno field.

The high mountains have always been home to eagles, hawks and falcons and it is not uncommon to see some species of birds of prey on a walk or hike almost anywhere in the country.

On the list of protected areas in Croatia are Dinara, the Neretva Delta, Mljet National Park, Plitvice Lakes National Park, Velebit, Biokovo Nature Park and many others. In Montenegro, important areas include Biogradska Gora, Durmitor, Prokletije, Ulcinj Salina and others. Protected areas in Slovenia include Lake Cerknica, Snežnik (plateau), Karst Plateau, Ljubljana Marshes, Trnovo Forest Plateau and Nanos.

ENVIRONMENTAL CONSIDERATIONS

Despite the beauty of the Dinarides, there has been irresponsible and negative impact on their natural resources during the transitional period, resulting from illegal exploitation and unplanned development. Climate change is the greatest threat to the delicate ecosystems of the high Dinaric area and the biggest impact will be on wildlife. Because of the impossibility of adapting to rapid changes to environmental conditions, plant and animal populations will disappear, and this will directly pave the way for the arrival of invasive species. Habitat conversion and loss is already occurring, primarily due to unplanned construction that fails to respect the limited resources of the area. Overexploitation, land and water pollution, deforestation and waste disposal are only a few examples of negative human impact. Enlarging protected areas is thus a serious and urgent issue, as the best way to protect the wildlife population is to protect their land.

LANGUAGE

There are three official languages spoken in Bosnia and Herzegovina: Bosnian, Croatian and Serbian. For the local people, there is a great importance attached to the name of the language. The differences are similar to those between American and British English. Bosnian, Croatian and Serbian are Slavic languages. Many words are similar in Czech or Slovakian, even Polish and Ukrainian. It is in the same family as Russian but is distinctly different.

In the Republika Srpska entity of Bosnia and Herzegovina many signs will be in Cyrillic, including road signs, which may make it difficult to know exactly where you are. In the Federation the Latin alphabet is mainly used. In the cities, it is very common to find English-speaking people; the heavy presence of the international community has almost made it a second language here. Most young people will have at least some knowledge of English almost anywhere you go.

Because of the large refugee and immigrant population that lived in Germany during the war there are many German speakers as well. In the rural areas, it will be hard to find English-speaking adults, but don't be surprised to find children able to 'small chat' with you in English. Some useful words and phrases can be found in *Appendix 1*.

VIA DINARICA ONLINE

For additional online content, articles, photos and more on Via Dinarica, why not visit **w** bradtguides.com/viadinarica?

2

Practical Information

THE VIA DINARICA TRAIL – A SUMMARY

Running the length of the Dinaric Alps from Slovenia to Albania, the Via Dinarica is the world's newest long-distance trail. The three trails – the White, Green, and Blue – are all linked by world-class hiking, biking and rafting routes, and provide opportunities for a huge variety of adventures for nature lovers and extreme sports enthusiasts alike. The Green and Blue trails are still being developed, but the main White Trail, which follows the highest spine of the Dinarics as it weaves through a large part of the western Balkans, is already operational. The natural wonders of the Via Dinarica are some of the most diverse, beautiful, and unexplored in Europe.

The Dinaric Alps may be Europe's best-kept secret for those drawn to the call of Mother Nature. The Via Dinarica long-distance trail links no fewer than seven countries through these majestic mountains that *National Geographic Traveler* has named as one of the 'Best of the World' in 2017. There are hundreds of wild, coursing rivers of crystal-clear turquoise hues, dramatic, rocky canyons and countless karst caves that compose the largest karst fields in the world. The Dinaric Alps range stretches fiercely across the western Balkans, offering challenging climbs up rugged peaks with epic views or gently rolling hills with wildflower-filled pastures as the mountains level off on the northern face of the range. These karst giants swell from the depths of the Adriatic Sea and rise steeply over the coast, and their rocky bases create crystal-clear waters not found anywhere in continental Europe.

From the coast, you can travel through a classic Mediterranean climate of sun-soaked vineyards and orchards into deep pine forests further north, and revel in the great diversity of ecosystems. On the Via Dinarica, the natural meets the cultural in enchanting ways. The still-thriving highland communities prove that no matter how remote you go, you're never terribly far from an adventure or a hot and hearty meal with a friendly local. Invading armies may have failed to conquer these mountains over the region's sometimes turbulent past, but the Via

Dinarica will lead you along footpaths that take you right to the heart of their magic. One of the most remarkable traits of the Via Dinarica, which sets it apart from other long-distance trails, is that it offers a rare glimpse into ancient cultures that have survived the manifold tests of time.

COUNTRIES OF THE VIA DINARICA

BOSNIA AND HERZEGOVINA

Capital city Sarajevo
Population 3.8 million
Language Bosnian, Croatian, Serbian
Currency Konvertible Mark (KM)
Area 51,197km²
Main Via Dinarica towns Jablanica, Mostar, Konjic, Sarajevo, Foča, Kalinovik, Tomislavgrad, Livno, Posušje
Highest peaks Veliki Vilinac (2,113m), Maglić (2,386m), Vran (2,074m), Zelena Glava (2,155m), Pločno (2,228m)
Length of Via Dinarica trail 327.8km (White Trail)
Activities Hiking, biking, rock climbing, caving, rafting, herb and berry picking, horseriding, skiing, fly fishing, canyoning

Bosnia and Herzegovina (BiH) is located in the heart of the Dinaric Alps, which rise steadily across the country from northwest to southeast, appearing in both Bosnia – the central and northern region of the country – and Herzegovina, the entire southern region. A huge portion of the Via Dinarica extends through this country's dramatically varying landscapes, including its characteristic karst fields, limestone mountains, lush valleys, primeval forests, alpine fields, crystal-clear rivers and green mountain lakes. The Dinaric mountain range is the natural boundary between the Mediterranean and continental climates, and BiH encompasses more of both climates than any other country along the Via Dinarica. Here, warm Adriatic temperatures clash with sometimes severe Alpine ones, producing one of the most diverse and unique ecosystems in all of Europe – in the central Herzegovina mountains alone, there are over 32 types of endemic species of flora and fauna. From the rugged peaks and rolling green hills of central and northern Bosnia to the dry and arid Mediterranean Herzegovina, this small land offers a more fascinating array of climates, cultures, vegetation, watersheds and wildlife than any other country in southeast Europe.

It is from this natural bounty that Bosnia and Herzegovina's rich cultural heritage has evolved. Creative and sustainable reliance on natural, local products is a tradition that has withstood the test of time and can still be observed throughout the country, especially in the

▲ Signage from the Our Lady of Sinj trail which overlaps with Via Dinarica in the far west of Bosnia and Herzegovina (OL)

mountain communities that the Via Dinarica trail enables travellers to explore. These customs feature exquisitely in local culinary culture, from the mountain herbs collected to make teas, *rakija* and natural remedies to the renowned mushrooms added to sauces and stews, the dried meats and organic cheeses, cream and yoghurt to the wild berries picked from sun-soaked Alpine fields. The hospitality along the way represents the pleasant, rustic and creative mountain culture that has emerged from this environment, connecting man and nature in ways rarely seen in modern times. While these mountain communities continue to preserve invaluable indigenous knowledge and heritage, they have been transformed by the Eastern and Western cultural flows at which BiH sits at the confluence. As you traverse this land on the Via Dinarica, you can observe archaeological and cultural remnants of the powerful empires that have laid claim to these mountains, forests and rivers, including the Roman, Ottoman and Austro-Hungarian to name just a few.

Trail information The White Trail in Bosnia and Herzegovina is perhaps the best marked of all the countries along the Via Dinarica. All information and GPS coordinates can be found on **w** viadinarica.com in English and the local languages. The entire 327.8km of the White Trail have both standard mountain markings as well as Via Dinarica signs and information boards. There are some tricky parts of the trail, including Prenj Mountain, but the entire trail is navigable.

ALBANIA

Capital city Tirana
Population 2.8 million
Language Albanian
Currency Lek (l)
Area 28,748km^2
Main Via Dinarica towns Valbona, Theth, Vermosh
Highest peaks Maja Jezerce (2,694m)
Length of Via Dinarica trail 45km (White Trail)
Activities Hiking, biking, skiing, rafting, kayaking, canoeing, fishing, spelunking, rock climbing, paragliding, birdwatching

Trail information Much of the Via Dinarica White Trail in Albania is well marked with local markings. There are several patches in the high mountains, however, where the trail markings seem to disappear. Good maps are available through the Peaks of the Balkans project, and meeting with the locals at Rilindja in Valbona or Prokletije National Park in Montenegro is always a good idea.

CROATIA

Capital city Zagreb
Population 4.2 million
Language Croatian
Currency Kuna (kn)
Area 56,594km^2
Main Via Dinarica towns/villages Zadar, Sinj
Highest peaks Veliki Zavižan (1,676m), Vaganski vrh (1,757m), Sveti Jure (1,762m), Sveto brdo (1,751m), Dinara (1,830m)
Length of Via Dinarica trail 556km (White Trail)
Activities Hiking, biking, rock climbing, snorkelling, scuba diving, paragliding, jet skiing

Trail information The trail in Croatia is quite well marked, however, there are several parts of the White Trail, particularly on Gorski Kotar, that are not so, and therefore not always easy to find. Go prepared with good maps and contact the Croatia Via Dinarica team at **w** viadinarica. hr for more information on those less-clear segments of the trail. At Paklenica National Park the trail 'ends' due to former frontlines and continues on asphalt road before rejoining mountain hiking routes.

MONTENEGRO

Capital city Podgorica
Population 676,872

Language Montenegrin, Serbian, Bosnian, Albanian, Croatian
Currency Euro
Area 13,812km^2
Main Via Dinarica towns Gusinje, Mojkovac, Plav, Kolašin, Žabljak, Plužine
Highest peaks Kom Kučki (2,487m), Planinica (2,330m), Bobotov Kuk (2,523m)
Length of Via Dinarica trail 243.6km (White Trail)
Activities Hiking, biking, rafting, rock climbing, snorkelling, scuba diving, paragliding, canyoning

Trail information The trail markings in Montenegro are very good. There is a cohesive trail system that extends throughout the northern part of the country that encompasses the Via Dinarica White Trail. Maps and coordinates can be found on **w** viadinarica.com.

KOSOVO*
Capital city Prishtina
Population 1.8 million
Language Albanian, Serbian
Currency Euro
Area 10,908km^2
Main Via Dinarica towns Peja, Rugova, Gjakova
Highest peaks Hajla (2,403m), Gjeravica (2,656m)
Length of Via Dinarica trail 120km
Activities Spelunking, hiking, biking, rock climbing

Trail information As the 120km of the Via Dinarica that lies within Kosovo* has yet to be fully integrated into the Via Dinarica White Trail, enquiries should be made through the Facebook page of Via Dinarica Kosova or the Kosovo Mountaineering and Alpinists Federation. Many trails are marked and connect to the Via Dinarica White Trail, but it is best to go with a local guide.

SLOVENIA
Capital city Ljubljana
Population 2 million
Language Slovenian
Currency Euro
Area 20,273km^2

*This designation is without prejudice to positions on status, and is in line with UNSCR 1244/1999 and the ICJ Opinion on the Kosovo declaration of independence.

Main Via Dinarica towns Postojna, Stari Trg pri Ložu, Ilirska Bistrica
Highest peaks Snežnik (1,796m)
Length of Via Dinarica trail 82.5km (White Trail)
Activities Hiking, biking, rock climbing, canyoning, paragliding, rafting, fishing, birdwatching

Trail information The trail markings in Slovenia are quite good throughout the country. The Via Dinarica White Trail is marked, but not with the standard Via Dinarica signage to be found elsewhere on the route. For further information, see the Via Dinarica White Trail map on the official website **w** viadinarica.com.

SERBIA
Capital city Belgrade
Population 7.12 million
Language Serbian
Currency Serbian dinar (din)
Area 77,474km^2
Main Via Dinarica towns Mokra Gora, Zlatibor, Nova Varoš, Sjenica
Highest peaks Pančićev Vrh (2,017m), Zlatar (1,627m), Kozji vrh (1,591m)
Length of Via Dinarica trail Green Trail, undefined
Activities Hiking, biking, rock climbing, canyoning, paragliding, rafting, fishing, birdwatching

Trail information Serbia is not a part of the Via Dinarica White Trail. The still-under-development Green Trail meanders through the country's southwestern mountain region, however, it is not yet fully marked as a coherent and continuous trail.

▼ Hikers in the highlands of Zelengora Mountain (KM)

WHEN TO HIKE

Summer is the most popular season for hiking and climbing in the Dinaric Alps, but the mountains are beautiful throughout the year. Owing to the complex climate influences at play in the region, the seasons vary in different parts of the chain.

WINTER A thick layer of snow covers most of the Central Belt during winter, and most local mountain roads are closed from October to May. For the adventurous of spirit, winter is a great time to hike the Dinaric Alps. It is the least crowded period, the snow can be walked upon after it hardens in January, and the air is the clearest. Winter is also a good time to climb the Maritime Belt, which is usually without snow, and is less crowded than at other times of the year.

SPRING Snow usually remains in the high mountains through the spring, but lower areas become more approachable beginning in March and April. On the coast and in lower Herzegovina, the sun warms the air quickly as spring begins. People swim in the Adriatic Sea as early as April – though, admittedly, mostly only the brave. Late spring is a wonderful time to visit anywhere in the Dinaric Alps, as the flora awakens, plants are in bloom, and light green shades begin to grace the woods and meadows.

SUMMER Summer (July–August) is the high season for outdoor activities. Most of the remaining snow melts away in June, and shepherds travel to their summer settlements high in the mountains. This is the time when most tourists visit the mountains, but because it is also the time when most locals travel to the coast, trails are not crowded. It can be very hot and sunny in the Dinaric Alps during the summer, especially in the Maritime and Northeastern belts, as in the Pannonian Plain, and a light mist can often obstruct the full distance of great views. In Mediterranean areas, be careful to carry enough water at all times, consider taking breaks during the middle of the day, and do not expect much shade or other relief from high temperatures. August is the month with the lowest average rainfall in high-altitude areas.

AUTUMN Early autumn is a lovely time to explore the Dinaric Alps. Temperatures cool but remain warm, forests become alive with colour and high mountain meadows turn golden-yellow. The weather changes in late autumn, which is by far the rainiest period, and is accompanied by pervasive fog. Mountain peaks remain under clouds for days or even weeks, and receive higher amounts of precipitation than lower areas. In November and especially in December, winter temperature inversions begin, which are characterised by higher air pressure pushing long-lasting cold fogs into the valleys and lowlands, leaving mountaintops clear and sunny – classic conditions for the Balkan ski season!

HIGHLIGHTS AND ROUTE PLANNING IN BOSNIA AND HERZEGOVINA

Listed below are a handful of highlights and don't-miss spots on the Via Dinarica White Trail in Bosnia and Herzegovina. Although there are impressive attractions along the entire route, most of them are located on stages 29–34 and 36–38.

BLIDINJE NATURE PARK Blidinje is the natural point to start the real trekking on the Via Dinarica White Trail from the west. Blidinje is a vast valley, with a beautiful lake, ski centre and Franciscan monastery. The hike up to Vilinac on Čvrsnica Mountain from here is steep but an exceptionally beautiful hike with many rewards at the top.

VILINAC Vilinac is a peak on Čvrsnica Mountain, where a small mountain hut of the same name is located. It can boast to having one of the best views to wake up to on the entire Via Dinarica in BiH. The hut is not open all year round so be sure to check for opening times and availability but it's definitely a hotspot to spend the night high up on the White Trail.

HAJDUČKA VRATA The 'Rebel's Door', as it's called, is a large, perfectly circular geological formation on the White Trail between Vilinac and Plasa on Čvrsnica Mountain. It's well worth the detour to scramble around on the rock formations and enjoy the stunning views of Diva Grabovica below and Prenj Mountain (the following stage on the White Trail) on the horizon.

PRENJ – HERZEGOVINIAN HIMALAYA Although Prenj Mountain is not the highest in the country, it is known to hikers as the mother of all mountains in Bosnia and Herzegovina. Its jagged peaks and daunting climbs have earned it the nickname of 'Herzegovina's Himalaya'. Hiking here is challenging and good navigational skills are necessary.

BORAČKO LAKE This semi-glacier lake is the reward after a challenging four days on Prenj Mountain. It is also accessible by car from the town of Konjic and is a good base from which to head either east or west on the Via Dinarica trail. It is a great swimming hole with plenty of accommodation facilities nearby, and is the location of many of the rafting operators who offer white-water rafting on the Neretva River.

LUKOMIR VILLAGE The White Trail passes through this ancient village, the highest and most isolated mountain village in Bosnia and Herzegovina. This quaint, medieval-style highland settlement is the perfect place to overnight and experience the highland cultures that have long faded from Europe's mountain communities. There is a beautiful mountain lodge that offers good accommodation and excellent food.

RAKITNICA CANYON From the Boračko Lake area all the way to the village of Umoljani, the White Trail follows the ridges of the Rakitnica Canyon, one of Europe's least-explored river canyons. The ridge walks along this 800m-deep canyon are world class and there are several access points for those with an adventurous spirit to scramble down to the river for a swim and to stare in awe at this raw beauty.

SUTJESKA NATIONAL PARK This place has been coined the 'Yosemite of the Balkans' with good reason. The park is home to the country's highest peaks and a rich population of wildlife. It is, however, best known for the Perućica Primeval Forest (one of two remaining in Europe) and for its historical significance. This is where Tito's Partisans broke through the Nazis in a decisive battle during World War II. The monument in the Tjentište Valley is a pilgrimage for many nostalgic former Yugoslavs.

NATIONAL PARKS AND PROTECTED AREAS

BLIDINJE NATURE PARK (Blidinje, Federation of Bosnia and Herzegovina; **e** info@blidinje.net; **w** blidinje.net) Blidinje is mainly composed of a visually stunning open valley called Dugo polje, situated between the great mountains of Čvrsnica (highest peak 2,228m) and Vran (highest peak 2,074m). Dugo polje, formed by glaciers off these two mountains, is exceptionally flat and holds the largest mountain lake in the country, Blidinje Lake. Thick forests of Bosnian pine cover the slopes of the bordering mountains, hiding Diva Grabovica, a narrow and deep gorge set in the foothills of Čvrsnica.

SUTJESKA NATIONAL PARK (Tjentište, Republika Srpska, Bosnia and Herzegovina; **☏** +387 58 233 200; **w** npsutjeska.info) Sutjeska National Park is proud of its history as the oldest and largest national park in Bosnia and Herzegovina. It was designated protected land in 1962, and has incredible natural heritage that is perhaps the most complex and diverse ecosystem in the region. The Strict Nature Reserve of Perućica is one of the few remaining primeval forests in Europe, and is home to the 75m-high Skakavac Waterfall. Zelengora Mountain has eight beautiful glacial lakes popularly called 'mountain eyes' as well as an abundance of endemic plant species. Situated in the national park, on the border with Montenegro, Maglić is the highest peak in the country at 2,386m. Another key attraction of the park is a remarkable communist monument at Tjentište. The Sutjeska River Gorge traces its way through all this, and is rich in brook trout.

DURMITOR NATIONAL PARK (BORDERING SUTJESKA NATIONAL PARK IN BIH) (Žabljak, Montenegro; \+382 20 601 015; w nparkovi.me/sajt/) In 1980, Durmitor National Park joined the UNESCO World Heritage List and is Montenegro's largest protected area. Shaped by glaciers, this park has numerous glacial features including valleys and lakes known as 'mountain eyes'. It is set along the Tara River Canyon, Europe's deepest gorge, which is remarkably free from dams or roads. It is known for hiking and mountaineering as well as rock climbing, rafting and canoeing. This land remains the home of indigenous farmers and shepherds who graze their animals on the high Alpine meadows and plateaus. Durmitor National Park is also home to old-grown European black pine forests as well as beech, fir and spruce, some of which grow up to 50m tall.

TOURIST OFFICES

VIA DINARICA SUPPORT CENTRE BIH (NGO Terra Dinarica, Vladimira Nazora 2, Sarajevo 71000; \+387 62 393 393; e info@terradinarica.com or viadinarica@viadinarica.com; w viadinarica.com) This is the best one-stop shop for all information on Via Dinarica that you need. This is the team that led the development project(s) and oversees the vast network of communities, service providers and mountain associations that make up the Via Dinarica. They can organise and advise on trip planning, provide information on trail conditions, connect travellers with local guides, and a vast range of other services aimed at providing timely and accurate information to travellers and to help local communities continue to develop the Via Dinarica.

OTHER ORGANISATIONS The main tourist organisations along the Via Dinarica in Bosnia and Herzegovina are:

Tourism Association of Federation of BiH portal w bhtourism.ba
Mostar Tourism Portal w turizam.mostar.ba
RS Tourist Organisation
Bana Milosavljevića 8, 78000 Banja Luka;
\+387 51 229 720, +387 51 231 670;
e tors@teol.net; w turizamrs.org

Herzegovina-Neretva Canton Tourist Board Dr Ante Starcevica bb, Mostar;
\+387 36 355 090; e hercegovina@hercegovina.ba; w hercegovina.ba
Konjic Municipality \+387 36 712 200;
e opcina.konjic@konjic.ba; w konjic.ba/index.php/o-opcini/turizam

Sarajevo Canton Tourism Association ☎+387 33 580 999; e office@sarajevo-tourism.com; w sarajevo-tourism.com
Foča Tourist Organisation Santiceva 16, Foča; ☎+387 58 212 416; e foca@yahoo.com; w focaravajuce.org

Kalinovik Tourism Organisation (w kalinovikturizam.com)
West Herzegovina Tourism Association Andrijice Šimića bb, 88320 Ljubuški; ☎039 830 062; e info@visithercegovina.com

The other countries through which the Via Dinarica trail runs have information on their respective tourist board and partner sites, as follows:

- Slovenia Tourist Board (w slovenia.info)
- Croatia Tourist Board (w croatia.hr)
- Via Dinarica Croatia (w viadinarica.hr)
- Montenegro Tourist Board (w visit-montenegro.com)
- Albania Tourist Board (w albania.al)
- Kosovo* Tourist Board (w beinkosovo.com)

TOUR OPERATORS

Information on the operators listed below and many more service providers can be found on the official Via Dinarica web page (w viadinarica.com).

Green Visions ☎(office) +387 33 717 290, +387 61 213 278; e sarajevo@greenvisions.ba; w greenvisions.ba. Green Visions is an ecotourism & outdoor adventure organisation based in Sarajevo. Their unique blend of adventure tourism & community development has made them a leading responsible tour operator in BiH & the Western Balkans. They focus on hiking, mountain biking, road cycling, snowshoeing, & insightful cultural trips along the Via Dinarica & throughout the western Balkans.

Lasta Travel Kralja Petra Krešimira IV 1; ☎+387 36 332 011; e travel@lasta.ba; w lasta.ba. Specialises in unique & authentic tours of Herzegovina for both groups & independent travellers. They offer superb service, excellent guiding, & one of the more original types of trips being offered in Herzegovina. One can visit little-known medieval graveyards, small vineyards in sleepy villages, as well as seeing & experiencing the more popular highlights of Herzegovina's Via Dinarica sections.

Via Dinarica Alliance e info@via-dinarica.org; w via-dinarica.org. The Via Dinarica Alliance is a co-operative of private adventure-tour operators. Members represent the countries throughout the Western Balkans & work together to offer six 8-day, cross-border tours along the trail. Green Visions (see left) is the representative for the Alliance in BiH.

Visit Konjic Donje polje bb, poslovni prostor 2, 8400 Konjic; ☎+387 61 072 027; e info@visitkonjic.com; w visitkonjic.com. This young but flourishing tour operator based out of Konjic runs mainly cultural tours in & around the Konjic area. They do offer rafting, hiking & village visits as well on the Via Dinarica section around Boračko Lake all the way up to Lukomir & Umoljani villages on Bjelasnica Mountain. They have very knowledgeable guides & operate the mountain lodge in Lukomir which is a must-see on the White Trail.

Zepter Passport (Green Trail) Veselina Masleše 8/I, Banja Luka; ☎ +387 51 213 394; e info@zepterpassport.com; w zepterpassport.com. One of the better travel agencies that organises tours & guides in the Krajina & in other areas of BiH for nature-based activities. They also arrange fishing trips. Zepter can arrange permits, gear rental & customs papers.

OTHER INTERNATIONAL TOUR OPERATORS ON VIA DINARICA
UK
Exodus w exodus.co.uk
KE adventures w keadventure.com
Regent Holidays w regent-holidays.co.uk

US
Bike tours.com w biketours.com
Mountain Travel Sobek w mtsobek.com
REI w rei.com
Wildland Adventures w wildland.com

Germany/Austria
Welt weit wander w weltweitwandern.at
Schultz reisen w schulz-aktiv-reisen.de
Ikarus reisen w ikarus.com

AGENCIES
Extreme Sports Club Scorpio Nurije Pozderca 11, Zenica; m +387 61 608 130;

e info@scorpio.ba; w scorpio.ba. Offers a wide variety of sports: rock climbing, mountain biking, paragliding, canyoning, hiking, ski touring & ice climbing.

Fikret's Hiking Adventures Malta 25, 71000 Sarajevo; ☎ +387 33 616 928; e fikret6@hotmail.com; ◻ FikretsHikingAdventures. Fikret is an independent guide who conducts hiking & city tours for those who have their own transport.

Limit (Green Trail) Džanića Mahala 7, 77000 Bihać; m +387 61 144 248; e lipa3@bih.net.ba; w limit.co.ba. Hiking & mountain-biking tours in the northwest town of Bihać near Una National Park.

Rafting and Hiking Club Encijan Kralja Petra bb, Foča; ☎ +387 58 211 150, +387 58 211 220; ☎ +387 65 626 588; e encijan@teol.net; w pkencijan.com. Encijan is a professional group of hiking guides & rafting skippers with a tradition of almost 15 years. They have bungalows & old mountain cottages along the Tara River for rafting accommodation. They are literally in the middle of nowhere.

Tudup Raft Polje Bijela bb, Mlin, Konjic; ☎ +387 36 287 008; m +387 61 628 573; w tudupraft.com. This outfit based out of Konjic offers a wide range of activities on the Via Dinarica. Their speciality is in the name, running rafting trips on the Neretva River, but they also do hiking, canyoning & other extreme sports around the Boračko Lake area. They have excellent guides & professional equipment.

RED TAPE

BORDER CROSSINGS Border crossings from Croatia to BiH are slightly different from the crossing(s) from BiH to Montenegro. Croatia is an EU member state and there are no agreements with BiH on mountain crossings for hikers. For this reason, the White Trail was developed to lead to the Croatian border at Kamensko where there is an official crossing. All through-hikers should use this crossing. Between BiH and Montenegro, there are two possibilities. From Sutjeska National Park it is possible to hike into Montenegro via Trnovačko Lake to summit BiH's highest peak, Maglić. The trail continues from there to Piva Lake and onwards towards Durmitor National Park. The border crossing from Prijevor in Sutjeska National Park to Trnovačko Lake may or may not be monitored by a border guard. It is a generally accepted practice that hikers can enter Montenegro to summit Maglić but it is expected that one returns to Sutjeska National Park after completing the climb. The official border crossing with Montenegro is in Šćepan polje where the Tara and Piva rivers join to create the Drina River.

MINISTRIES OF THE COUNTRIES OF THE VIA DINARICA

Ministry of Foreign Affairs Bosnia and Herzegovina Musala 2, Sarajevo 71000; ☏ +387 33 281 100; e info_mvpbih@mvp.gov.ba; w mvp.gov.ba; ⏰ 09.00–17.00 Mon–Fri

Ministry of Foreign Affairs Slovenia Prešernova cesta 25, SI-1001 Ljubljana, PP 481; ☏ +386 1 478 2000; e gp.mzz@gov.si; w mzz.gov.si; Consular services: Šubičeva 10, 1001 Ljubljana; ☏ + 386 1 478 2305

Ministry of Foreign Affairs Croatia Trg NŠ Zrinskog 7–8, 10000 Zagreb; ☏ +385 1 4569 964; e ministarstvo@mvep.hr; w mvep.hr; ⏰ 08.00/09.00–16.00/17.00 Mon–Fri

Ministry of Foreign Affairs Montenegro Stanka Dragojevića 2, Podgorica; ☏ + 382 20 416 301; e kabinet@mfa.gov.me; w mvpei.gov.me/en/ministry; ⏰ 09.00–17.00 Mon–Fri

Ministry of Foreign Affairs Serbia Kneza Miloša 24–26, 11000 Belgrade; ☏ +381 11 361 6333; e mfa@mfa.rs; w mfa.gov.rs; ⏰ 07.30–15.30 Mon–Fri

Ministry of Foreign Affairs Kosovo* MFA Bldg, Str'Luan Haradinaj' pn, 10000 Prishtina; e mfa@rks-gov.net; w mfa-ks.net; ⏰ 08.00–16.00 Mon–Fri

Ministry of Foreign Affairs Albania Bulevardi Zhan D'Ark, 1000 Tirana; ☏ +355 69 982 6678; e DK@mfa.gov.al; w punetejashtme.gov.al; ⏰ 08.00–17.00 Mon–Fri

GETTING THERE AND AWAY

BY AIR The main airport in Bosnia and Herzegovina is **Sarajevo International Airport** (w sarajevo-airport.ba). There are also international airports in **Tuzla** (w tuzla-airport.ba) and in **Mostar** (w mostar-airport.ba). In neighbouring Montenegro there are airports in **Podgorica** and **Tivat** (for further information, see w montenegroairports.com). Croatia has several international airports, including **Franjo Tuđman International Airport**

*This designation is without prejudice to positions on status, and is in line with UNSCR 1244/1999 and the ICJ Opinion on the Kosovo declaration of independence.

(**w** zagreb-airport.hr) on the outskirts of Zagreb, **Split International Airport** (**w** split-airport.hr), the international airport of **Dubrovnik** (**w** airport-dubrovnik.hr) on the southern coast, and the airport in **Rijeka** (**w** rijeka-airport.hr) situated on the northern coast and the most convenient airport for the Slovenian starting point of the Via Dinarica trail.

Connections are mainly through European cities and can be somewhat limited, so check them carefully well in advance of planning your trip. From London, there are direct flights to Ljubljana and Zagreb, but you would need to make a transfer to fly to Sarajevo, Podgorica or Tirana. If a quick stop in Italy sounds appealing, the Friuli Venezia Giulia international airport in Trieste is minutes from the Slovenian and Croatian borders, and not far from the northern starting point of the Via Dinarica White Trail.

BY RAIL There are trains between London and Ljubljana several times a day, but none is direct – a minimum of two train transfers will be required. The trip will range from 18 to 22 hours, and cost between €155 and €500. There are direct lines from Ljubljana to Austria, Italy and Germany. The railway station in Zagreb is also reasonably well connected, with direct lines to Italy, Germany and Hungary. You will generally find better connections by bus in this region, though train tickets may be cheaper.

Reserve tickets well in advance to reduce costs. Train schedules may be reduced on weekends and holidays. If you would like to travel more through Europe by train, consider getting an InterRail Pass (**w** interrail.eu) or Eurail Pass (**w** eurail.eu), which must be bought outside Europe.

🚃 Sarajevo Railway Station
(Željeznička stanica Sarajevo) ☎ +387 33 655 330; **w** zfbh.ba

🚃 Ljubljana Railway Station
(Železniška postaja Ljubljana) ☎ +386 1 291 3332; **w** slo-zeleznice.si

🚃 Zagreb Railway Station (Zagreb Glavni kolodvor) ☎ +385 1 3782 532; **w** hzpp.hr

🚃 Podgorica Railway Station
(Željeznička stanica Podgorica) ☎ +382 69 811 674; **w** zcg-prevoz.me

🚃 Tirana Railway Station The station is currently under construction; however, Podgorica in Montenegro is actually closer to the Via Dinarica trailhead in Albania than Tirana.

BY BUS Getting around the Balkans by bus is cheap and easy; the only potential obstacle is having to wait a while for a bus to arrive. Even very small towns in this region are connected by bus.

Regional hubs
Sarajevo w busbosnia.com
Mostar w busbosnia.com
Ljubljana Bus Station w ap-ljubljana.si

Zagreb Bus Station w akz.hr
Rijeka Bus Station w autobusni-kolodvor.com

Split Bus Station w ak-split.hr   **All Croatian stations** w buscroatia.com
Podgorica Bus Station w busterminal.me

BY CAR This is the easiest way to get around the Balkans, if you already have access to a car. The roads in Slovenia and Croatia are very good; further south, highways almost disappear and local roads are mountainous and curvy, and almost always only one lane.

The main European highways that will take you to the Dinaric Alps are:

- Milan/Rome–Venice–Trieste–Split–Dubrovnik–Skadar/Skhodra
- Stuttgart–Munich–Salzburg–Ljubljana
- Frankfurt–Nürnberg–Linz–Graz–Zagreb–Split
- Budapest–Zagreb–Rijeka
- Budapest–Osijek–Sarajevo–Mostar
- Belgrade–Kraljevo–Podgorica

PUBLIC TRANSPORT

Public transportation in the cities and towns of the Via Dinarica in BiH is efficient and inexpensive, not least because they are all relatively small. **Buses** are a cheap and convenient way to get around Bosnia and Herzegovina with almost all towns being connected, though asking a local (or the bus driver) for help may be your best way to get information on in-town bus routes. Tickets to ride city buses and trams can be bought from the driver of the vehicle, or from any pavement kiosk around town; they cost between 2KM and 4KM, depending on the city. The regional bus hubs, used for international or long-distance trips, are listed opposite. Although the bus network is extensive, if you are travelling in the more remote parts of the country, you may have to wait up to a day for a bus to come through.

A **train** service runs from Sarajevo to Mostar daily and stops in Konjic and Jablanica, which are both on the Via Dinarica White Trail.

Taxis are much cheaper in BiH than in western Europe or North America, and unlike in many of those cities today, you can hail taxis on the street, and don't have to look for a taxi rank. Because cities and towns are small and traffic only really exists in the capitals during rush hour, taxis are a very convenient mode of public transportation in the Balkans.

ACCOMMODATION

Accommodation along the Via Dinarica can vary widely. You'll occasionally need to set up a tent along the trail, but you will find that you can sleep with a roof over your head on most nights. Some accommodation types are self-serviced, meaning the only service they may offer is running water, but there are also many cosy houses and inns that offer home-cooked food and beds in private rooms. There, you will always meet the warm hospitality Bosnia and Herzegovina is famous for.

Hotels and **motels** exist in small cities and towns that the trail passes near. Private rooms, private bathrooms with towels, Wi-Fi and restaurants are always part of the deal. As with all other listed types of accommodation, payment may be accepted in cash only. Along the Via Dinarica rooms cost between 30KM and 60KM but can be significantly more expensive in Sarajevo and Mostar.

Pansions are small inns with private rooms. They are similar to households, but are run more like a business. Pansions almost always have Wi-Fi and decent bathrooms, though bathrooms are not always connected to private rooms. They offer home-cooked food, towels and bedding, and a cosy atmosphere. Rooms cost between 20KM and 60KM.

Households, also called **guesthouses**, are private houses that offer comfortable accommodation in the form of small dormitories or private rooms. They have restaurant areas where they serve home-cooked comfort food, and offer an ambience of traditional, 'ethno-style' Balkan character. They have decent bathrooms, electricity, and sometimes have Wi-Fi, but they are more rustic than a hotel. Rooms cost between 10KM and 60KM.

There are several **horse farms** along the Via Dinarica Trail that provide accommodation. Most of them also offer guided horseriding excursions on or near the Via Dinarica Trail.

▼ Outback camping on the White Trail (AB)

Private huts are privately owned small mountain facilities. Some do welcome hikers and guests. Most of the private huts on the Via Dinarica site are available for rent.

Mountain lodges are run by local mountaineering clubs and sometimes organise hiking or other group activities from the lodge. Sleeping areas are usually communal dormitory rooms, sometimes with bunkbeds, other times just with space for sleeping bags. They usually include some services such as functional kitchens and bathrooms, but don't always have electricity, and often don't have Wi-Fi. Many mountain lodges are not accessible by car. Mountain lodges will charge a moderate fee for an overnight stay.

Shelters are the most rustic type of accommodation you'll find along the trail. They are usually wood or stone shacks that keep out the wind and rain, but little else. They tend to be small buildings with space for five or ten sleeping bags, maybe a bathroom hut in the vicinity, but no kitchen, running water, or restaurant services. Shelters are often right alongside the trail, and can only be reached by walking. Accommodation in shelters is free.

There are no proper campsites on the Via Dinarica White Trail in Bosnia and Herzegovina. **Camping** is officially not permitted but is regularly practised on the Via Dinarica. Be sure to follow basic camping etiquette and be extra safe with campfires. Food should be stored safely away from wild animals.

EATING AND DRINKING

One of the Via Dinarica's many unique features is that, unlike other hiking trails that go through remote wilderness, there are frequent opportunities to have a hot meal right along the trail. Because there are countless ancient villages nestled within the nooks and crannies of the Dinaric Alps, the trail offers a real introduction to local lifestyles, including local cuisine as well as the characteristic warm hospitality. Highland food is the truest expression of Balkan food: heavy in bread, heavy in meat, and as local and fresh as can be. Portions tend to be large, and finishing your plate is always considered a sign of good appreciation to the host. Vegetarians may find it challenging to find meatless main dishes, as even some vegetable soups are cooked in meat broth. Bean stew is, however, very popular and very common.

Bread	*Kruh/Hljeb*	Meat	*Meso*
Fried dough	*Uštipci*	Lamb	*Janjetina*
Savoury pie	*Pita*	Veal	*Teletina*
Beans	*Grah/Pasulj*	Chicken	*Piletina*
Soup	*Supa/Juha*	Vegetables	*Povrće*
Stew	*Čorba/Juha*	Salad	*Salata*

▲ A traditional highland breakfast of fresh cheese, homemade bread and jam, and a strong 'kafa' or coffee (EO)

Drinking along the Via Dinarica is also a unique experience. Its defining feature is the famous local alcohol, **rakija**. This drink, usually translated to English as brandy, is a distilled hard alcohol made from a great variety of fruits and other plants that are prevalent in the Dinaric Alps. Some very common flavours include plum, pear, apple, quince, mixed herbs and honey. You might be offered *rakija* at every meal, no matter the time of day, as it is considered a natural remedy for many ailments and a great source of vitality when hiking. Your hosts will often join you in a glass of *rakija*, in another expression of the convivial hospitality of the Balkans. **Beer** is also a part of the drinking culture, but with less tradition, and usually less variety. Another interesting traditional drink that you will come across at mountain restaurants is **kiselo mlijeko** (sour milk) which is a thick, *very* natural yoghurt that pairs well with salty dishes such as *pita* and *uštipci*.

MONEY

The countries of the Via Dinarica White Trail use the following currencies: the Konvertible Mark (KM) in **Bosnia and Herzegovina** (exchange rate: €1 = 1.95KM – fixed); the lek (l) in **Albania** (€1 = 133l); the kuna (kn) in **Croatia** (€1 = 7.54kn); and the euro in **Slovenia**, **Montenegro** and **Kosovo***. (Exchange rates from November 2017.)

*This designation is without prejudice to positions on status, and is in line with UNSCR 1244/1999 and the ICJ Opinion on the Kosovo declaration of independence.

There are ATMs in the larger towns along the route, but do not count on passing an ATM very frequently. Besides basic necessities, accommodation and travel costs, the only thing you should have to pay for in the Dinaric Alps will be entrance to national parks, but only for some of them. You can pay by card at most grocery stores, hotels and restaurants, but more often you will encounter small businesses that accept local cash only. That said, most of the accommodation and food along the trail is very cheap, so you should not have to carry large amounts of cash at any time. Be sure to always have some money with you in case of an emergency; if possible, try to carry smaller bills, as not every establishment will be able to break a 100KM, or even a 50KM, note.

BUDGETING

Besides plane tickets, gear, and any other major preliminary costs, your Via Dinarica experience will not cost you very much if you stick rigidly to the trail. If you spend a night in anything other than your tent or a shelter, it will cost between 10KM (€5) and 50KM (€25) . Food will range from 10KM (€5) to 20KM (€10) per meal, and an alcoholic drink will cost no more than 4KM (€2) to 8KM (€4). Local transportation is very affordable, and buses are the cheapest and easiest option. Hitchhiking is still common in the Balkans, but we advise against it unless you speak the local language very well, or are travelling with a local. You may want to hire a guide for certain segments of the trail, or spend a day getting to know a place by undertaking a different activity, such as by joining a white-water rafting or canoeing tour. These activities will cost about 50KM (€25) to 100KM (€50) per day.

TELEPHONE NUMBERS AND MOBILE PHONES

INTERNATIONAL AND LOCAL AREA CODES There are five international dialling codes (country codes) relevant to the Via Dinarica White Trail.

Bosnia and Herzegovina +387
Slovenia +386
Croatia +385

Montenegro +382
Albania +355
Kosovo* +383

These numbers are followed by a local area code, the initial zero of which you should only dial if calling from inside the country. In Part One this guidebook, numbers are listed with their country codes, for calling from an international location or non-local phone. When calling from a local phone, disregard the country code and add a zero before the local area code. Part Two of this book uses just the local numbers.

For emergency phone numbers, see page 39.

MOBILE PHONES Mobile coverage is good for most of the trail, but it may be hard to find a signal in remote areas. Charge your smartphone at every opportunity, as you cannot expect to have electricity access every day. You can buy a local sim card to avoid international calling fees.

INTERNET

Most hotels have free Wi-Fi, but mountain huts and shelters often do not. You can find internet cafés in many towns along the trail. If carrying a smartphone, make sure you download the Via Dinarica Outdoor Active map app before beginning the hike (**w** viadinarica.com).

PUBLIC HOLIDAYS AND FESTIVALS

The following are the main holidays observed in Bosnia and Herzegovina. Expect banks and most shops to be closed on holidays, and public transport to operate a reduced Sunday timetable, or not at all.

1–2 January	New Year
6–7 January	Orthodox Christmas
Spring	Good Friday
Spring	Catholic Easter Sunday & Monday
Spring	Orthodox Easter Sunday & Monday
1 May	Labour Day
Varies	Eid al-Fitr/Ramazanski Bajram
Varies	Eid al-Adha/Kurban Bajram
1 November	All Saints' Day
25/26 December	Christmas/Boxing Day

FESTIVALS
July
Baščaršija Nights Festival Throughout July, there are cultural events and festivals in Sarajevo.
Mostar Rock and Blues Festival Outdoor and indoor rock and blues concerts in Mostar in mid-July.

August
Sarajevo Film Festival Set in mid-August, this is the largest film festival in the region, founded in 1995.

September
MESS Fest MESS is a contemporary theatre festival that takes place in Sarajevo from late September to early October each year.

November

Jazz Fest Jazz Fest takes place in Sarajevo every November, and makes good use of Sarajevo's edgy jazz bars. Shows range from small, intimate gatherings at the dimly lit Pink Houdini, to big bands at the larger Monument Bar, to electro-jazz concerts in the theatre of the Bosnian Cultural Centre.

OUTDOOR ACTIVITIES

HIKING Although the Via Dinarica has every variety of outdoor activity, its first and foremost function is as a long-distance hiking trail. From leisurely day hikes to epic Alpine adventures, the Via Dinarica is a demanding hiking trail. The main White Trail that runs from Albania to Slovenia is a 1,350km long-distance trail. The world's newest trail, it is truly wild, with many sections that travel through remote areas with only basic shelters for accommodation. The trail is, however, designed along popular routes lined with mountain huts, shelters, and small private homestays in most locations. The hiking terrain ranges from family-friendly hiking to very challenging mountaineering, and always offering a little bit of something for everyone. The White Trail offers top-notch hiking through some of the most pristine wilderness areas in all of Europe. Whether it be the long trek across Velebit in Croatia, the humbling hike up and over Prenj Mountain in Bosnia and Herzegovina, or the steep ascent to the Accursed Mountains on the border of Montenegro and Albania, the Via Dinarica truly represents the best of European hiking. It is no exaggeration to say that this is the most bio-diverse area in all of Europe, with a rich diversity of landscapes, remote wilderness, and a peek into old-world Europe found in the highland culture of the Dinaric Alps.

MOUNTAIN BIKING Mountain biking is an exhilarating, adrenaline-pumping way to devour the highlands more quickly and daringly than on foot, and the rapidly changing landscapes along the Dinaric Alps are exciting to experience pedalling along at high speed. Though not the tallest mountains in the world, the Dinarides offer variable and challenging terrain, such as steep wooded slopes that open out into breezy expanses with views to deep valleys below, and uniquely jagged summits with rock formations that fascinate and impress. These mountains are characterised by a diversity of climates as they act as the barrier between warm, sunny Mediterranean lands on their south-facing slopes, to the colder, more Alpine areas on the continental side. Alongside the movement to improve and create new hiking trails in the Dinaric Alps has been a similar initiative for mountain-biking tracks, which often follow

▲ Caving on Stage 27 in the world's largest karst field (MS)

or intersect the Via Dinarica trail. There are now tracks that delve deeply into the wilderness of this enchanting mountainous region, and they're accessible and easy to follow. The biking trails in Bosnia and Herzegovina even made *National Geographic*'s list of Top 10 adventure destinations in 2012.

CAVING As home to the largest karst field in the world there is no lack of caving adventures to be had on the Via Dinarica trail. Although spelunking, or pot-holing, is certainly a niche activity, there is no place on earth that has a more intricate and diverse underground cave system than the Dinaric Alps. One can enjoy open caving in commercial caves such as Vjetrenica in Herzegovina or Postojna Cave in Slovenia or opt for the more challenging endeavours deep into the belly of the earth in places like Livanjsko Fields in western Bosnia and Herzegovina which has been identified as the largest single karst area on planet earth. Commercial caving is safe and easily accessible in many locations along the Via Dinarica. Caves are open to visitors all year round except for during extreme weather conditions. Spelunking is offered by several clubs in Slovenia, Croatia, Serbia and Montenegro, where proper safety gear and guides are recommended.

WATERSPORTS The Dinaric region has some seriously impressive waterways. Less is scientifically known about most of the hundreds of rivers in this region than about many rivers in the more remote Amazon Rainforest. But one thing is for certain – these sparklingly clear waters offer some of the most attractive **white-water rafting** and **kayaking** in the world. For **angling** enthusiasts, the entire region offers world-class **fly-fishing** for trout and grayling. **Canyoning** is a challenging sport to say the least but for the hard-core the canyoning experiences to be had on the Via Dinarica are second to none. If it's a saltwater experience you're looking for, **sea kayaking** on the Croatian and Montenegrin coast is second to none. Watersports are a popular pastime for adrenaline junkies and novices alike along the waterways of the Via Dinarica. The many rafting routes comprise a full range of difficulty levels, and while some must be sought out from deep within the lush wilderness of the Dinaric Alps, others are found conveniently close to major towns. Many rafting routes travel along or across the Via Dinarica trails, which bring a welcome and refreshing break from the demands of hiking the trail. The Dinaric Alps region is home to the largest karst field in the world, and its rivers have carved dramatically beautiful gorges through the limestone mountain range. You can cruise upon turquoise waters with walls of rock or trees rising on either side of you, manoeuvring through thrilling white-water cascades or gliding along peacefully, enjoying the scenery. Whichever way you choose to experience this eco-friendly adventure sport, you're sure to have a blast. More information on watersports in the region can be found on the official Via Dinarica website (**w** viadinarica.com).

WHAT TO SEE AND DO

GASTRONOMY Food in this part of the world is, by and large, organic by default. This region continues to enjoy an abundance of small-scale, local agriculture, and while urbanisation is on the rise, rural communities and farms are thriving. Healthy, free-range livestock is the norm as are natural and robust fruits and vegetables, including what might be the best tomatoes in the world. Dishes are simple but hearty, savoury and full of flavour, and alongside the fresh vegetables you're likely to have a variety of rich cheeses, crispy, fried *uštipci*, and succulent, slow-cooked meat. There is great pride in the quality of these natural goods, and the preparation and enjoyment of food is a well-respected art and tradition that always builds closeness and conviviality between those who partake. The same can be said about the art of drinking in the Balkans, whether it be coffee or the local firewater known as *rakija*. Both are vital parts of every society in the region. Most deals – love, business, or otherwise – are done over a drawn-out cup of coffee, a glass of Mediterranean wine, or a strong *rakija*. As with food, all these are locally produced, and usually made using age-old traditions. Part of the Via Dinarica experience is enjoying the finer things in life, and eating and drinking certainly top the list.

VILLAGE LIFE While urbanisation is occurring here as it is everywhere in the world, Dinaric village life persists – and looks quite similar to how it did hundreds of years ago. The Via Dinarica will take you hiking or biking through hills in which charming villages are tucked away in spectacular natural settings, where you can experience the warmth of small communities – and of their traditionally made stews and breads. The mountainous conditions of the Dinaric Alps have powerfully shaped the livelihoods of village dwellers, and the harmony that these communities struck with their nature has withstood the test of time. Fundamentally tied to the land, village life in the Dinaric Alps makes full, sustainable and creative use of the natural wealth abounding all around. This is a display of the connection between humans and nature in a way rarely seen in Europe today, and an active preservation of indigenous knowledge that is well worth supporting.

CULTURAL HERITAGE Like anywhere else, the natural environment in the Dinarics has influenced the culture of the region. For thousands of years, the Dinaric Alps have provided local inhabitants refuge from invaders from both the east and west, creating space where uniquely Dinaric heritage could thrive amid the confluence of opposing forces that has occurred in this region, which has been known throughout history as a crossroads of cultures. The traditional architecture, dress, food preparation and ceremonies are well preserved in the highlands, offering a rare experience of old-world customs in Europe. Much ancient history is scattered across the mountains, such as the UNESCO-protected ancient necropolises of *stećci* gravestones that sit on remote Alpine slopes. Archaeological sites also remain standing in towns that have been centres of culture for centuries, marked by hundreds of medieval settlements or ruins in the high mountains along the Via

▼ Medieval tombstones at Čengića Bara lie on a hillside just south of Kalinovik on a variant of stage 35 (OL)

STEĆCI

Stećci are the mysterious medieval tombstones found throughout Bosnia and Herzegovina and across its borders in Croatia, Serbia and Montenegro. These tombstones that dot the countryside are a testament to the rich cultural and natural heritage of ancient Alpine settlements in the Dinaric Alps. For this reason, they were nominated and declared UNESCO World Heritage Sites in 2016. They can be found in many locations along the Via Dinarica trail, including Umoljani, Blidinje and Kalinovik on the BiH section of the White Trail. Stećci are often found in pristine natural settings, whether perched on scenic ridges or incorporated into beech-tree forests, and represent the best-preserved and genuine artistic expression of this form of medieval sepulchral art. In the areas where they emerged and evolved, they reflect permeation of various cultural influences of the time (from the second half of the 12th to the 16th century), and they belong both to the Catholic West and the Orthodox East. Although immersed in the medieval European culture, the historical context and specific regional space where we find them, with traces of earlier influences (prehistoric, ancient and early medieval), stećci, by several aspects, remain a unique phenomenon in the medieval European artistic and archaeological heritage. Their main specificity is precisely in their number, over 60,000 in Bosnia and Herzegovina and 10,000 in Croatia, Montenegro and Serbia combined – and not recorded anywhere else in Europe.

Dinarica. If you're looking for a break from the trail and want to explore the towns and cities connected to the Via Dinarica, the sites and sounds will not disappoint. Whether it be the Ottoman charm of Sarajevo, the jaw-dropping beauty of Dubrovnik and Kotor, or the countless raw and authentic towns in the lower valleys, there is an impressive repertoire of cultural heritage to explore.

TRAVELLING WITH KIDS

Many parts of the Via Dinarica trail are extremely remote, so be sure to do detailed research before heading out on any given route. In the central part of the White Trail (stages 33 and 34), the terrain is suitable for hiking with kids. In and around the village of Umoljani (stage 34) there is very good access, well-marked trails, and plenty of places to rest, eat and enjoy the surroundings with the little ones. For teenagers who have some hiking experience, Sutjeska National Park (stage 37) has some fantastic hiking from the Suha Valley up to Prijevor and on to Trnovačko Lake.

▲ Crossroads of the Via Dinarica in Blidinje Nature Park (OL)

MAPS AND APPS

The best way to research the Via Dinarica is through the official website (**w** viadinarica.com), where the entire White Trail is mapped with coordinates. Each stage of the trail can be printed into a small pocket guide if need be. The app is part of the Outdoor Active (**w** outdooractive. com) network and all the White Trail stages and information can be found on their app. On all major intersections of the Via Dinarica White Trail in Bosnia and Herzegovina there are codes on trail signage that will indicate exactly where you are and what waypoints are nearby. There are no commercially prepared walking maps available for the stages of the White Trail in Bosnia and Herzegovina. Some mountain associations have maps of their particular mountains, but these are generally not for sale.

TRAIL MARKINGS

The Via Dinarica White Trail in Bosnia and Herzegovina is very well marked, however, in the other countries of the White Trail this is not necessarily the case. While fewer waymarkings maintain the environment in its natural state, this does mean that you will have to use your own navigational skills from time to time. For unmarked areas, prepare your GPS maps well in advance, and when mapping information is scarce, you may also have to ask for help from locals. The standard markings in BiH are a red circle with a white middle. The Via Dinarica signposts are to be found on the entire length of the White Trail and are depicted opposite.

EMERGENCY PHONE NUMBERS

The European emergency number 112 is used in all countries of the Via Dinarica White Trail. These calls are free of charge and operators should speak local languages and English. The operator will be able to connect you to some of the other emergency services listed below.

BOSNIA AND HERZEGOVINA

European emergency number	112 (includes emergency medical services & mountain rescue services)
Police	122
Fire Department	123
Ambulance	124
Civil Protection	121

BORDERING COUNTRIES
Croatia

European emergency number	112 (includes emergency medical services & mountain rescue services)
Police	192
Fire Department	193
Ambulance	194
Emergency at sea	195
Road help	1987

Montenegro

European emergency number	112 (includes emergency medical services & mountain rescue services)
Police	122
Fire Department	123
Ambulance	124

MOUNTAIN RESCUE

Mountain rescue services can be reached through the 112 general emergency phone line. They are usually run by brave and dedicated volunteers, so please only call them in cases of true emergency. Mountain rescue services are free of charge. If you do need to call a mountain rescue service, be prepared to supply the following information:

- Your name and the name of anyone injured
- Description of the incident
- Location of the incident, including altitude or other coordinates
- Time of the incident
- Weather conditions and visibility

BOSNIA AND HERZEGOVINA   Mountain rescue stations in the Dinarics:

- **Mountain Rescue Service Foča** (**m** +387 66 776 465; **e** gssrsfoca@ hotmail.com)
- **Mountain Rescue Service Sarajevo** (**m** +387 62 654 456; **e** gss@gss-sarajevo.com; **w** gss-sarajevo.com/index.php/prijava)
- **Herzegovinian Mountain Rescue Service Mostar** (**m** +387 62 339 333; **w** gss-mostar.com)
- **Mountain Rescue Service Konjic** (**m** +387 60 330 0800; **f** gss.konjic)
- **Mountain Rescue Service Jablanica** (**m** +387 61 043 241; **e** gss. jablanica@gmail.com; **w** gssjablanica.com.ba)
- **Mountain Rescue of Canton 10** (for Livno) (**m** +387 63 112 233; **e** info@gss-hbz.com; **w** gss-hbz.com)

BORDERING COUNTRIES

Croatia **Croatian Mountain Rescue Service** – Hrvatska gorska služba spašavanja (HGSS) (in Croatian only) (**w** gss.hr). The following mountain rescue stations are either in, or close to, the Dinarics: Rijeka, Split, Šibenik, Zagreb, Ogulin, Delnice, Karlovac, Pula, Gospić, Samobor, Zadar, Makarska, Dubrovnik.

Montenegro **Mountain Rescue Service of Montenegro** – Gorska služba spasavanja Crne Gore (GSSCG) (in English and Montenegrin) (**** +382 40 256 084; **e** gsscg@gss-cg.me; **w** gss-cg.me). The following mountain rescue stations are either in, or close to, the Dinarics: Žabljak, Kolašin, Nikšić.

LONG-DISTANCE HIKING: TRAVELLING LIGHT   *Rudolf Abraham*

Hiking a distance of approaching 330km, the weight and comfort of the gear you choose – footwear, rucksack, clothing, etc – will make a huge difference to your enjoyment of the Via Dinarica White Trail. Since you won't need to carry a tent, sleeping bag/mat, etc, or any food beyond a snack for any given stage, you can manage to pack quite light. While those with plenty of experience of long-distance hiking routes will have their own tried and trusted gear, for those less familiar with hiking a route this long, the following list should prove useful.

CAMPING GEAR There are a few stages on the Via Dinarica where little or no accommodation is available so packing a light tent (in warmer season) and lightweight sleeping bag is recommended. It's always best to carry a small (gas) cooker on the route regardless of the availability of accommodation. Nights in the mountains can be quite chilly even in the summer, with temperatures sometimes reaching single digits (°C) in higher-altitude areas. A waterproof lining for your tent is always sensible as keeping dry is vital for any mountain outing.

▲ Belgian hikers enjoy the views from Maglić (KM)

RUCKSACK Along with footwear, this is the single most important piece of gear in terms of how comfortable – or not – your whole experience of hiking the Via Dinarica is going to be. As you won't need to carry overnight equipment, a pack size of around 40 litres should be ample. Whether you prefer a pack with lots of external side pockets or none is a personal choice; personally, I prefer none as I just see them as more zips to break and seams to leak. In any case, aim to get a pack that weighs not much more than around 1kg, and that has an internal frame – many smaller packs have no frame, which makes them much less comfortable to carry. The best-designed, most comfortable lightweight pack I've used is the Fastpack 50 made by Lightwave (w lightwave.uk.com), a small UK company. It is 50 litres, but the compression straps make it perfectly suitable for carrying a smaller load; there's also a 40-litre version, which weighs in at just over 1kg and has an extremely comfortable frame.

HIKING BOOTS/SHOES Heavier hiking boots are great for ankle support; however, the climate and terrain along the Via Dinarica are both mild enough that lightweight hiking shoes are sufficient, and in being considerably lighter will save you umpteen kilojoules of energy expenditure.

TREKKING/RAFTING SANDALS As well as providing a change of footwear in the evenings at the end of a stage (especially if it's been raining and your boots need to dry), these can make a welcome change from hiking boots/shoes on a hot day over easy terrain. I swear by Keen Newport H2 sandals, which are wonderfully comfortable, lightweight and hard-wearing, with a chunky enclosed area to protect your toes (**w** keenfootwear.com). Open-toed hiking sandals are all very well but leave you susceptible to stubbing your toe on a large chunk of rock at some point – a remarkably painful and often spectacularly bloody experience, which I can confirm is best avoided. If you want to cut down weight even further, take a pair of flip-flops instead.

RAINPROOF JACKET As on any mountain hike, carrying a waterproof, breathable shell should be considered mandatory. There are plenty of fabrics around – Gore-Tex, eVENT, etc – some more breathable than others, of varying weights and cuts. The best lightweight jacket I've tried is the Minimus Grand Tour made by Montane (**w** montane.co.uk), an amazingly lightweight and breathable piece of kit which weighs in at under 500g and packs down to the size of a large orange.

SOFTSHELL JACKET Warm, preferably windproof softshell (Polartec PowerShield or similar material) jacket or mid layer.

LIGHTWEIGHT BASE LAYER A couple of long-sleeved (more versatile than short-sleeved) hiking tops with thermal/wicking properties. The Factor 1 Plus (top and leggings) and Factor 2 thermal base layers made by Sub Zero (**w** subzero.co.uk) are by far the best and the most effective I've used. In fact, the Factor 2 top is warm enough that during the summer you could ditch carrying a fleece jacket.

HIKING TROUSERS Lightweight, quick-drying material, either with or without zips to convert them into shorts. Páramo's Maui II (**w** paramo-clothing.com) are exceptionally comfortable and hard-wearing, and have outdone any other pair of hiking trousers I've owned.

WALKING SOCKS Wearing good-quality hiking socks (cushioned at different points around the foot) helps avoid blisters – and counters the need to wear two layers of socks or sock-liners. For all but winter use, a mid- or lightweight hiking sock will be sufficient on the Via Dinarica. Bridgedale (**w** bridgedale.com) is a good brand to go for in the UK.

TREKKING POLES Using trekking poles will make an enormous difference to your knees over a distance of 330km. When carrying trekking poles in your checked-in luggage on your flight (they're usually prohibited from hand luggage) *always pack them inside your rucksack*, preferably at the centre or against the back frame, rather than on the outside – trekking poles can be damaged easily and one good knock from a large suitcase would bend them and thus render them utterly useless. (If they're too long to fit inside your pack, carefully remove the upper from the lower sections of the poles, which will make them a little shorter, and keep the internal locking mechanism in place by wrapping a rubber band around it several times; it's also worth wrapping something around the pointed ends to prevent it tearing anything in your pack, or the pack itself.)

WATER FILTER Chances are you won't really need a water filter on the Via Dinarica, since you can fill flasks at your pension/mountain hut each morning before setting off. However, the Sawyer Mini (**w** sawyer.com) is such an astonishingly good piece of kit – tiny, weighing in at a mere 56g, and all you have to do is screw it on to a plastic water pouch and squeeze to have instant purified water – that I carry it on any hiking trip, to have the flexibility of refilling at springs along the way.

WATER BOTTLES Either a lightweight aluminium flask such as those made by Sigg, and/or collapsible plastic pouches/bladders such as those made by Sawyer (see above), Platypus, etc, which weigh almost nothing and take up no space in your pack when they're empty. Plastic mineral water bottles are liable to break/split if dropped, or after several days in a pack – disastrous if they're inside your pack at the time, annoying at the very least if they're not, and you're several hours away from the next available water – and potentially contribute to landfill, since they may or may not end up in recycling. I prefer to carry several Sawyer pouches (2l and a couple of 1l) and a Sigg flask. Aim to carry two litres of water per person per day.

SMARTPHONE The Via Dinarica app is part of the Outdoor Active (**w** outdooractive.com) network and all the White Trail stages and information can be found on this app.

SMARTPHONE CASE Take a waterproof, shock-proof phone case – since you'll be using the app often enough, possibly in pouring rain, over rocky terrain, your phone (and ultimately you, if you drop it) will be much happier if protected in a decent case. LifeProof makes good phone cases for outdoor use, waterproof and shockproof without being too bulky (**w** lifeproof.co.uk).

COMPASS Doubtless you'll have one on a smartphone as well, but having a backup in case your phone dies or the battery runs out is essential – as is knowing how to use it.

TORCH/HEADLAMP Headlamps, such as those made by Petzl (**w** petzl.com), are best since they leave your hands free. While a small headlamp such as the Petzl Tikka is fine for most use, if you get benighted somewhere on the trail and actually need a light for route finding, it won't be sufficient – you'll need something more powerful (160+ lumens).

SUN PROTECTION Sunhat, preferably with a roll-down flap around the back and sides to protect your neck, such as the excellent Summer Cap made by Páramo (**w** paramo.co.uk), sunglasses and sun-block (SPF factor 20 or higher).

TOWEL Essential in some mountain huts, so carrying a small, lightweight and quick-drying travel towel such as those made by Páramo (**w** paramo.co.uk) is a good idea.

SLEEPING-BAG LINER A sleeping-bag liner or sheet sleeping bag is required for staying at some mountain huts but not all. Silk sleeping bag liners are lighter (weighing around 125g), pack up very small and are slightly warmer; cotton sheet sleeping bags are cheaper and cooler but considerably bulkier and weigh more (350g or more).

SMALL FIRST-AID KIT Containing at a minimum: two knee-support bandages (get these before travelling, don't wait until you need them on the route); fabric plaster strip for any blisters (Hanzerplast is the best one I know of, and doesn't come off wearing boots all day); non-stick wound dressings; small scissors, Swiss Army knife or similar (for cutting fabric plasters); alcohol wipes; small roll of surgical tape; tick remover. If you don't want to make up a kit yourself, Care Plus makes them in a range of sizes (**w** careplus.eu). There are several 'blister repair kits' available such as Second Skin, although avoiding blisters in the first place (by wearing good-quality footwear and socks) is arguably the best form of blister protection there is.

OTHER ITEMS In addition to the above, you may wish to add a lightweight synthetic- or down-filled waistcoat (which will give much more warmth in ratio to its bulk than an extra fleece) for cooler evenings, such as the Torres Gilet made by Páramo (**w** paramo.co.uk). If you're hiking early or late in the year a lightweight pair of gaiters will be useful where there's snow (Keela makes good lightweight gaiters; **w** keela.co.uk), and slightly heavier-weight hiking socks.

Other essentials include warm gloves and hat (even in the summer); emergency reflective bag or 'space blanket'; whistle (for attracting attention in an emergency); Swiss Army knife, Leatherman tool or similar;

small two-pin adaptor (220V/50Hz). A lightweight, quick-drying, long-sleeved 'travel' shirt, T-shirt and underwear should complete the clothing you need and are likely to actually wear.

Reliable outdoor equipment specialists, with branches throughout the UK, include Blacks (**w** blacks.co.uk) and Cotswold (**w** cotswoldoutdoor. com). Needle Sports (**w** needlesports.com) and Tower Ridge (**w** towerridge.co.uk) are both excellent online suppliers (the former also has a store in Keswick). However, most of the larger high-street chains like Cotswold don't carry many of the small, ultralight brands mentioned here. The best places to shop for ultralight hiking gear are Backpacking Light (**w** backpackinglight.co.uk) and Ultralight Outdoor (**w** ultralightoutdoorgear.co.uk).

SAFETY IN THE MOUNTAINS *Rudolf Abraham*

The stages of the Via Dinarica vary in difficulty and often stray deep into wild areas far from any settlements or 'civilization'. This means that a simple slip or sprain or a sudden change in weather has the potential to leave you stranded on high ground, possibly overnight, and anyone venturing into the mountains should be aware of the possible dangers, be prepared to administer basic first aid, and know how to react in an emergency. As with any mountain walking destination, the following basic precautions should always be observed:

▼ Suspension bridge crossing over the Neretva River near the village of Kašići on stage 33 (KM)

- Leave a description of your itinerary with someone at home, and before you leave the hut or hotel you've stayed in tell someone where you're walking to that day.
- Do not set off on high or exposed routes in bad weather.
- Always carry adequate warm and waterproof clothing.
- Always carry a small first-aid kit (page 44) and an emergency bag or 'space blanket', a torch, and a whistle for attracting attention.
- Always carry an adequate supply of water to prevent dehydration, as well as some food.
- Always carry sufficient navigation aids – whether compass, GPS, smartphone, and the relevant map(s) – and know how to use them.
- Know the internationally recognised call for help: six visual or audible signals (torch, whistle, etc) per minute, followed by a minute's pause, then repeated. The answer is three signals per minute followed by a minute's pause.
- Know the emergency signals to rescue helicopters: both arms raised above the head means YES, help required, one arm raised above the head with the other extended downwards means NO, help not required.
- In cold or extreme weather conditions, be alert to any of the symptoms of exposure or hypothermia – loss of co-ordination, slurred speech, numbness in hands and feet, shivering, shallow breathing or impaired vision. If hypothermia is suspected, get the victim out of the wind/rain, replace wet clothing with dry garments, keep the victim warm and give hot fluids and foods with high sugar and carbohydrate levels.
- If you are taking out a travel insurance policy, make sure it covers hiking and accidents in the mountains (many don't).

DEHYDRATION Make sure you carry enough water to avoid becoming dehydrated – two litres per person per day should be sufficient.

HYPOTHERMIA Hypothermia, meaning a dangerous loss in body temperature, is generally caused by cold and/or wet, windy weather conditions, insufficient warm/waterproof clothing (page 42), and exhaustion. If not treated it can lead to death. Be alert to any of the symptoms of hypothermia – see above.

WILD ANIMALS The rugged and sparsely populated wilderness of the Dinaric Alps is home to an abundance of animal life. There are several types of large, predatory carnivores you should be aware of when hiking, including bears, wolves, lynxes and wildcats. None of them poses much of a threat to humans, and attacks on anything other than sheep or goats are almost unheard of – they usually want to avoid you more than you want to avoid them! The main habitats of bears, wolves and lynxes in this region are the Alpine forests of the high Dinarics from Slovenia, across Croatia and Bosnia and Herzegovina to the border with Montenegro. Bears are more dangerous in the spring, as mother bears can get aggressive in looking out for their cubs. Wolves are more dangerous in winter, when they descend from the cold, most remote areas of the mountains into warmer areas near the Dalmatian and Montenegrin coast hinterlands, lower Herzegovina, and continental parts of Slovenia, Croatia, Bosnia and Herzegovina, Montenegro, Albania and Serbia. Snakes are another animal that hikers should watch out for. They can be found anywhere along the Mediterranean and in the Dinaric Alps. Generally, they do not pose much of a threat either, but try to watch your step and be vigilant when picnicking.

TICKS Ticks are prevalent in the undergrowth along the Via Dinarica. Ticks should ideally be removed as soon as possible as leaving them on the body increases the chance of infection. They should be removed with special tick tweezers that can be bought in good travel shops. Failing that you can use your finger nails: grasp the tick as close to your body as possible and pull steadily and firmly away at right angles to your skin. The tick will then come away complete, as long as you do not jerk or twist. If possible douse the wound with alcohol (any spirit will do) or iodine. Irritants (eg: Olbas oil) or lit cigarettes are to be discouraged since they can cause the ticks to regurgitate and therefore increase the risk of disease. It is best to get a travelling companion to check you for ticks; if you are travelling with small children, remember to check their heads, and particularly behind the ears.

Spreading redness around the bite and/or fever and/or aching joints after a tick bite imply that you have an infection that requires antibiotic treatment, so seek advice.

MINES Landmines and other explosive remnants of war (ERW) from the Balkan wars of the 1990s are a risk that must be taken seriously when hiking in the Dinaric Alps. Minefields remain in certain places in the region, with the majority in Bosnia and Herzegovina and many in Kosovo* and parts of Croatia. Almost all potential mined areas are known and marked off. Warning signs include red signs that say 'mine' or 'МИНЕ' (Cyrillic), signs with skull and crossbones, plain red signs, and occasionally an upright stick with a red cloth tied to the top. The Via Dinarica carefully avoids and gives a wide berth to all mine-suspected areas, is a tried-and-tested route and hence very secure. It is, of course, wise to stay on the trail as much as possible.

*This designation is without prejudice to positions on status, and is in line with UNSCR 1244/1999 and the ICJ Opinion on the Kosovo declaration of independence.

Updates on the landmine and munition situation in each of the countries of the Via Dinarica trail can be found at (**w** the-monitor.org).

There are also mine action centres in Bosnia and Herzegovina (**w** bhmac.org) and Croatia (**w** www.hcr.hr/hr/index.asp), which have up-to-date and detailed information on the situation in the country.

EXTREME WEATHER CONDITIONS Climates clash in the Dinaric Alps, which are the high-altitude transition point for the warm Mediterranean climate of the Adriatic coast and the cool Alpine climate of the high Dinarics. Expect sudden changes in temperature and weather conditions when hiking in this area, especially along the Maritime Belt and parts of the Central Belt. Expect also a high level of precipitation. The karst topography is both a blessing and curse in this sense, as its porousness not only stops flooding but also prevents rain-accumulation water sources in the mountains.

LOW-IMPACT TREKKING *Rudolf Abraham*

If people destroy something replaceable made by mankind, they are called vandals; if they destroy something irreplaceable made by God, they are called developers.

Joseph Wood Krutch

▼ Hikers near the remote village of Čuhovići on Bjelašnica Mountain (KM)

48

Large numbers of visitors inevitably place a degree of strain on the environment, from trail erosion to waste management. At the risk of sounding pedantic and stating the obvious, I would like to flag up the following to Via Dinarica hikers:

STICK TO ESTABLISHED TRAILS Walking on either side of an established trail simply widens it, increases erosion and damages surrounding plant life (and Alpine plants can take several years to recover from a single human bootprint). Please stick to marked trails, and don't take short cuts. Occasionally trails are clearly diverted to let an area recover; please follow these diversions.

NEVER LIGHT OPEN FIRES High temperatures in the summer frequently combine with a lack of rain and the presence of dry winds, leaving forests and grasslands tinder-dry, and easily ignited by a carelessly discarded cigarette. Owing to the risk of forest fires you should *never* light an open fire in the wild.

DON'T PICK WILDFLOWERS Obviously. They look far nicer growing in the wild anyway.

CARRY ALL LITTER OUT OF WILDERNESS AREAS Please don't leave litter in the wild – and this includes any litter bins you may find at various spots along the trail, by a picnic spot or a picturesque mountain lake. While someone will come and empty these at some point, in the meantime you have no control of this litter being blown off by the wind or dragged off by wildlife. Take all your litter out of the wild (after all, it doesn't weigh much by that stage) and dispose of it sensibly in a town.

LEAVE GATES AS YOU FIND THEM If you find a gate closed, then shut it again after you've passed through. Leave an open gate open, as the farmer may have left it like that for a reason.

WILD CAMPING Camping is possible in national parks and other protected areas and is not strictly regulated or prohibited. There are few proper campsites on the route but wild camping is usually permittable in unpopulated areas.

USE TOILETS AT PENSIONS, HUTS AND RESTAURANTS It takes several months for toilet paper to fully decompose; use the toilets at pensions, huts and restaurants, otherwise always bury toilet waste 15cm underground. Do *not* burn toilet paper.

▲ The summer highland settlement of Gradina near Umoljani Village on stage 34 (m/S)

DON'T BUY BOTTLED WATER There's simply no need to buy bottled water – the tap water is fine to drink all along the Via Dinarica, and bottles create waste, not all of which is going to be recycled. Carry a small filter such as a Sawyer Mini (page 43) if you want to top up at springs along the route.

BUY LOCAL PRODUCE WHERE POSSIBLE In doing so, you will support small businesses and the local economy.

USEFUL LINKS

w viadinarica.com
w the-monitor.org
w via-dinarica.org
w viadinarica.hr
w dinarskogorje.com

3

Gateway towns
and trail access points

Tim Clancy

GATEWAY TOWNS

There are a handful of gateway towns and cities along or near the Via Dinarica White Trail in Bosnia and Herzegovina. The capital Sarajevo is the main international transport hub and there you can find everything you might need either before or after long-distance hiking. Mostar is the main city in the southern region of Herzegovina and is well connected to other destinations on the White Trail; it is easily accessible from Croatia as well. The other gateways towns are much smaller but all offer places to relax, restock hiking supplies, or just take a day off from the trail to soak up the local culture. The access points to the White Trail all have at least basic infrastructure, are well marked, easily accessible and are the best places to start the hiking journey on the Via Dinarica White Trail.

TOMISLAVGRAD Although there isn't much going on in this sleepy western Bosnian town, it is a good base to buy supplies or chill out before heading on to the Via Dinarica. Tomislavgrad is just across the border from the Croatian leg of the White Trail. The largest storage lake in Europe, **Buško jezero** (Buško Lake), whose surface covers 57km², borders the town. For anglers, there are more fish than one can handle. The wind from the long valleys of **Livanjsko polje** and **Duvanjsko polje** (Livanjsko and Duvanjsko fields) provides optimum conditions for parasailing. Water skiing, rowing and canoeing are among the watersports that the tourism association here is developing. You can camp along the banks of the lake, and in nearby wooded areas. Tomislavgrad is also the gatekeeper to **Blidinje Nature Park**: the park entrance is marked from the outskirts of town towards **Lipa**. Don't let the dirt track confuse you; good roads connect a large portion of the park. **Grabovica Eco-Village** (pages 71–2) is located on Buško jezero near the border with Croatia, where the Bosnian Alpine and Dalmatian–Mediterranean climates intersect at an altitude of 700m and **Lovre** (page 78), which lies north Bukovica and about 10km south of Tomislavgrad, offers inexpensive accommodation and meals. **Bošnjak household** (page 72), about 10km west of Tomislavgrad, offers accommodation for tourists and hikers visiting Buško Lake and the caves around Prisoje village.

Regular **buses** to Tomislavgrad travel from Livno and Mostar.

MOSTAR The Via Dinarica skirts the city of Mostar to both the east and the north. It's safe to say that the UNESCO World Heritage Site of the **Stari most** (Old Bridge) has always been the main attraction in Mostar. However, few know that Mostar is 88% mountain terrain, including the Via Dinarica White Trail.

The old town is very compact and is ideal for a walking tour and most of the main tourist sites can be seen in one day, including a number of

▼ Mostar's Stari most (Old Bridge) is a UNESCO World Heritage Site (L/S)

fine examples of Ottoman architecture. There are also several museums and churches well-worth visiting.

Mostar is one of the must-see destinations in Bosnia and Herzegovina, so if you're going to take a break from the Via Dinarica this stunning city is certainly worth the while.

Shopping in Mostar is oriented around the tourist economy. Several cobblestone streets in the heart of the old town, to the immediate left and right of the Old Bridge, are crammed with shops selling a wide array of souvenirs, ranging from kitschy to authentic, hand-crafted items. Most of these shops are open from early morning until late evening.

As there are as many cafés in Mostar as there are pubs in London, it's never difficult to find a cool spot to take a break from the hot Herzegovina sun. The old town has an enticing quality, particularly on the Neretva, which encourages you to sit for hours and just soak up the sights and sounds. Unlike in most tourist places in the world, café and restaurant owners in Mostar will never ask you to leave, even if you've been sipping a Turkish coffee for 2 hours.

Restoran Picerija Megi (Kralja Tomislava 29; **w** megi.ba; mains 15–20KM); has a tasty Italian menu, and **Taurus** (Kriva ćuprija 4; mains 12–20KM) is a traditional restaurant near the Kriva ćuprija. For something lighter try **Grill & Sandwich Bar Jimm** (Staro Veležovo; **f** jimmmostar; mains 6–12KM).

For its relatively small size, Mostar has a good range of hotels, bed and breakfasts, and hostels. Consider the stylish Motel Emen (**w** motel-emen.com; from 80KM pp per night) or the larger **City Hotel** (**w** city-hotel.ba; 90KM pp per night). Cheaper options include the family-owned **Pansion Botticelli** (**w** villabotticelli.com; 50KM) and **Pansion Kriva ćuprija** (**w** hotel-mostar.ba; from 90KM pp per night), which is just 100m from the Old Bridge.

Mostar has a small **airport**, with only scheduled flights to a few destinations, and is around a 3-hour drive from the larger airports at both Split and Dubrovnik. With two **bus** stations, the city is well served by public transport. The M-17 road is the main access route from Sarajevo to Mostar, via Konjic and Jablanica. The **train** service from Ploče (on the Adriatic coast in Croatia) to Sarajevo has a stop in Mostar, but has not been running in full service for some time. **Taxis** are plentiful in Mostar but the city is compact and easy to get around on foot.

Tourist information Mostar Tourist Information Office (Rade Bitange 5 (old town); ☎ 036 580 275; w turizam.mostar.ba; ⊕ May–Oct 09.00–noon daily) is, of course, the best source of information for visitors, and provides the best-available short guide *Mostar and its Surroundings*, with a short summary of the city's history, culture, art, things to see and do, and many outstanding photographs. It also has a useful colour tourist map.

JABLANICA In the Alps in Austria or Switzerland a place like Jablanica would be a mountain resort town. Instead, here, it remains a tiny town with little or no developed mountain tourism. But things are changing. Jablanica now sits right on the path of the Via Dinarica White Trail. Nestled on a terraced plateau below the intimidating peaks of **Prenj** and **Čvrsnica mountains**, it is the natural connecting point between two of the most challenging sections of stages on the White Trail.

The **Neretva River** carves its way through the centre, dividing the massive mountain ranges. It was at Jablanica that the Partisans won an unlikely victory in World War II, in the **Battle of the Neretva**. The bridge that the Partisans downed and cleverly escaped over with 4,000 wounded still hangs from the high cliffs as a reminder of one of their greatest victories. The **War Museum** is just next to the bridge, and an old German bunker on the east side of the river has now been converted into a restaurant and café.

Apart from this famous battle, Jablanica is known for *jagnjetina* (roast lamb). On the main road south of town are the trademark restaurants that have made Jablanica a place at which most locals, and those passing through, have spent some time. There are more than ten such restaurants, each selling the exact same thing: lamb by the kilo. If you are having trouble choosing which to stop at, **Zdrava voda** (mains 20KM) is certainly one of the nicest, as is **Restoran Kovačević** (mains 20KM). There is one decent hotel in town, the **Motel Hollywood Jablanica** (m 062 604 578; 30KM pp per night) located in the centre of the town.

Jablanica is easily reachable by **train** from either Sarajevo or Croatia. The Sarajevo–Ploče and Sarajevo–Zagreb trains both stop at Jablanica station. There are several **buses** daily from Sarajevo to Mostar, stopping in Jablanica. A Zenica–Dubrovnik bus stops here, too. Almost all buses from Mostar or Međugorje to Konjic or Sarajevo stop in Jablanica. Coming from Sarajevo by **car** it will take you around an hour and a half to drive the 86km on the M17 to Jablanica. From Mostar, it is 53km.

Tourist info can be found in Jablanica at Bitka za ranjenike bb (☎ 036 757 151; e t.zajednicajab@bih.net.ba).

See page 100 for a town plan of Jablanica.

KONJIC This is yet another Herzegovina town nestled between two of the Via Dinarica White Trail's mountain ranges. Konjic is an exciting place because of the wilderness adventures happening left, right and centre. The Neretva River running through town, and Prenj Mountain hovering behind, dominate the town. One of the best things to see here (and shop around in) are the family-owned woodcarving shops: Konjic has long been known for its wood craftsmen.

There are several recommended places to stay and eat. The **Hotel Oaza** (**w** hoteloazakonjic.com; 45KM (single room), 10KM for breakfast) is only 100m from the Old Konjic Bridge. The **Motel Konak** (**w** hotelkonak. ba; 50KM B&B), also next to the Old Bridge, has comfortable rooms and an excellent restaurant. The **Han** restaurant (Donje polje bb; mains 15–20KM) looks like a modern villa and is hard to miss. The modest **Regional Museum** stages rotating exhibitions and provides an interesting glimpse into the way people lived through the ages. **Tito's Bunker** (Hadžića polje; **m** 061 918 324, 061 072 027; ⏱ by appointment only, via phone) is only 10–15 minutes from Konjic by car and is by far one of the most exciting attractions in the area.

Konjic is well connected by **train** with both Sarajevo and Croatia. The Zagreb–Sarajevo–Ploče line goes through Konjic station once per day. There is no official **bus** station in Konjic to call or buy tickets. Most buses coming from Sarajevo to Mostar or Jablanica will stop at

▼ An old Ottoman bridge spans the Neretva River in the town of Konjic (AB)

the city's main department store. Coming from Sarajevo by **car**, follow the signs to Mostar; it takes around an hour to drive the 64km to Konjic. From Mostar, it is 74km on the M17, going through Jablanica and Ostrožac.

SARAJEVO Sarajevo is the capital city of Bosnia and Herzegovina and a gateway to all sections of the Via Dinarica White Trail in BiH. If there is one place in continental Europe that symbolises the crossroads between East and West, Sarajevo would have to be it. From the oriental Ottoman-style quarters lined with sweet shops, cafés and handicraft workshops, to the administrative and cultural centre of Austro-Hungarian times, to the socialist-era housing blocks with their everyday neighbourhood feel, playgrounds and small businesses, Sarajevo encompasses a variety of worlds in one small valley.

Sarajevo is a city that feels like home.

Hotels in the city are generally mid-range in price. Pansions, or smaller guesthouses/bed and breakfasts, dominate the accommodation market, particularly in the old town.

▼ Sarajevo is a fascinating mélange of east and west, mountains and plains, urban and rural (AB)

Situated in the centre of town, the **Hotel Colors Inn Sarajevo** (**w** hotelcolorsinnsarajevo.com; rooms 100–140KM pp per night) embodies the charm of the city itself, but if you're looking for something quieter try **Pansion Kandilj** (**w** kandilj.com; 80–100KM pp per night), which has cosy rooms and a lovely Ottoman sitting room. Two hostels are worth mentioning: **Hostel Vagabond** (**w** vagabond.ba; 30KM pp per night), in the central pedestrian zone of Ferhadija Street, and **The Doctor's House** (**w** thedoctorshousehostel.com; 30–40KM pp per night), which is a short walk uphill from the main cathedral in the old town.

Eating in Sarajevo has always been a tasty and affordable experience. The cuisine may not be super sophisticated, but it is exceptionally tasty. For the budget traveller or lover of street food, there is an abundance of cheap, local fast-food places serving hearty portions, but be aware that many restaurants are closed on Sundays. Try **Barhana** (Đulagina čikma 8; mains 10–18KM), a Sarajevo institution, hidden in a courtyard off the main walkway in Baščaršija, **Pod Lipom** (Prote Bakovića 4; **w** podlipom.ba; mains 8–15KM), a traditional restaurant serving all the classic Bosnian dishes, or **Dveri** (Prote Bakovića 12; **w** dveri.co.ba; mains 12–22KM), which serves excellent cuisine, including great soups and homemade breads.

Sarajevo has an ancient tradition of handicrafts in leather, metal, wood, textiles, shoes, gold, carpets and rugs. Gift and souvenir shops are in abundance in the old town and there are a few fabulous little shops around town that sell all-natural or organic local products.

The city is the main transportation hub in the country, with the largest international airport with regular daily flights from over a dozen destinations. It is easily accessible by air, bus, rail or car, with the airport only 20 minutes from the city centre. The **rail** and **bus** stations are also conveniently situated in the city centre (a second bus station is located in the east of the city), the latter with an extensive network of routes both internationally and within BiH. **Buses** to Zagreb usually take 6–8 hours, Split 7–9 hours, Dubrovnik and Belgrade both 5 hours and Mostar 2.5–3 hours. The local bus system is run down, but is the best in the country. **Trams** and **trolleybuses** are also a reliable means of transportation around the city. The **rail** system in BiH is modest at best, with old and slow rolling stock, but it can be a great way to see the countryside if you are not in a hurry. Travelling by **car**, Bosnia and Herzegovina has only a few four-lane roads, which does slow one's progress, but from Sarajevo one can, with relative ease, access the Via Dinarica White Trail in Sutjeska National Park, Umoljani village and Boračko jezero (Boračko Lake). All of these access points are around a 90-minute drive from the city centre. **Taxis** are fairly inexpensive in Sarajevo, with stands located all over the city and operating 24/7. **Walking** in Sarajevo is a local pastime, as the compact city centre and old town make it easy and enjoyable to do most moving around by foot.

For more detailed information on where to stay and eat, what to see and do, and how to best get there and away, please see the *Bradt Travel Guide to Bosnia and Herzegovina*.

Tourist information Sarajevo's only **tourist information centre** (☎ 033 580 999; **e** tourinfo@bih.net.ba; **w** sarajevo-tourism.com; ⊕ 09.00–16.00 Mon–Fri, 10.00–14.00 Sat–Sun) is located on Sarači in the old town and provides information for hotels, museums, excursions, city tours and other activities. There is also a *Don't Miss Sarajevo* guide as well as an *In Your Pocket* guide. The website **w** Sarajevo.travel/en promotes tourism in and around Sarajevo. The **Sarajevo Navigator** (**w** navigator.ba) has information points all around town, and also produces *Navigator*, a monthly what's-on guide.

FOČA Foča is quite a nice little town on the edge of the mighty **Drina River** only 75km southeast of Sarajevo. The Ćehotina River flows through the town and feeds the Drina. The surrounding mountains are wild and beautiful, and wildlife teems in the dense forest towards the Montenegrin border. Hunting and fishing are popular sports in this region, and besides being a main town close to the Via Dinarica, Foča is also the gathering point for rafting on the Tara. Foča is also close to two of the most beautiful places in Bosnia and Herzegovina: the Tara River Canyon and Sutjeska National Park, which should not be missed.

There are several places to stay and eat. The **Hotel Zelengora** (Nemanjina 4; **e** info@hotel-zelengora.com; 48KM pp per night) is a relic from Yugoslav times. The **Motel Brioni** (Solunskih dobrovoljaca 2; \058 210 646; 42KM B&B) has simple rooms and is a very pleasant place for a meal on the riverbank. The **Konoba Zlatna Dunja** (Njegoševa bb; mains 8–15KM) serves as a true representation of the cuisine of eastern Bosnia, made the 'old way'. The **Monte Cristo Pizzeria** (Njegoseva bb; mains 8–15KM) is a comfortable and good-value option.

For local advice, visit the **tourist information centre** (Tourism Organisation of Foča; Šantićeva 16; \058 212 416; **e** to.foca@yahoo.com; **w** focaravajuce.org; ⊕ 08.00–15.00 Mon–Fri).

A few **buses** run daily between Sarajevo and Foča, most from the bus station in east Sarajevo, but a couple from the city's central bus station, taking around 2 hours.

Tara River Coined the 'jewel of Europe' (by the locals of course), this wild, turquoise-blue river is a raging mass of water fed by the towering mountains of **Durmitor National Park** in Montenegro. The Tara River traverses the border of Bosnia and Herzegovina and Montenegro, rising from the mountain ranges in the north of Montenegro and flowing 140km, meeting the **Piva River** and forming the **Drina**, one of the longest and largest rivers in the Balkans.

For eons, the powerful flow of the Tara River has hollowed out a soft limestone surface, creating the sculpted form of gorges and chasms that we see today. Age-old earth erosion has created the 82km-long canyon, 1,300m at its deepest and the second largest in the world after the Colorado.

Along the river's banks the vegetation is very dense, containing a large number of tree species, with the black pine forests of special interest. *Crni pod*, or the black floor, is home to unusually tall trees. Some reach as high as 50m and are more than 400 years old.

Aside from nature lovers and fishermen, the river also attracts a large number of adrenaline junkies. Rated at level 3–5, the river offers some of the most intense and challenging rafting in Europe. Most groups operate out of Foča (pages 58–9; there are also several rafting agencies in Montenegro) and offer breakfast, lunch and overnight camping in their rafting packages.

The **Rafting Center Drina-Tara** (Bastasi bb; **w** raftingtara.com; rooms from 15–30KM) is an excellent location for anyone planning a rafting trip, with comfortable rooms and traditional meals. Most of the guides and skippers are trained professionals. **Camp Hum** (Bastasi bb; **m** 066 491 993; **e** rezervacije@rafting-tarom.com; rooms 20–30KM pp) has double- or multiple-bed rooms, an excellent restaurant and a sauna. Rafting companies include: **Highlander** (**w** highlandertim.com); **Rafting Club Drina-Tara**; **Rafting Club Encijan** (**w** pkencijan.com); **Rafting Club Montings** (**w** tararafting.net); **Rafting Club Tara 87** (**w** kamptara87.com); and **Tara-raft** (**w** tara-raft.com).

The Tara River is best approached from Foča with a guide: the small dirt tracks along the river on the Bosnian side are unclear and it is easy to get lost. The easiest approach is from Durmitor National Park in Montenegro, but that requires border crossings and more directions. Foča is accessible from the south via Trebinje–Gacko–Sutjeska National Park if you are coming from the coast or Herzegovina. From Sarajevo, the main southeast route via Trnovo and Dobro polje leads directly to Foča.

VIA DINARICA HUBS

There are several locations situated along the 350km or so of the Via Dinarica White Trail in Bosnia and Herzegovina that have been designated as hubs, chosen for their infrastructure, accessibility and geographic location. These hubs are good starting, resting or finishing points for those who plan on doing certain stages or sections of the trail. All four hubs have information provision, accommodation and access to and from the trail. At the far west end of the trail, near the Croatian border, is **Blidinje Nature Park**. It is the best starting point into the highest mountains and most attractive part of the Via Dinarica White Trail on Čvrsnica and Prenj mountains. In the central part of the trail, near the town of Konjic, is **Boračko jezero** (Boračko Lake). It is a good resting spot after a challenging Prenj Mountain hike and an excellent launch spot for rafting on the Neretva River or continuing northeast on the Via Dinarica towards Sarajevo. **Umoljani** is a small village on Bjelašnica Mountain near Sarajevo, with good access from the capital via asphalt road. One can take good day hikes here or continue on the Via Dinarica in either direction – south following the Rakitnica Canyon towards Boračko jezero, or east towards the Ljuta Valley and the town of Kalinovik. **Sutjeska National Park**, at the far east of the trail on the Montenegrin border, has significant infrastructure and some of the most beautiful hiking on the entire Via Dinarica trail. There is easy access from the park, which has facilities both in the Tjentište Valley below the high peaks of Maglić and Zelengora mountains, as well as mountain accommodation at both ends of the park.

▲ The Via Dinarica White Trail is 350km of hiking trail through mostly pristine wilderness (m/S)

BLIDINJE NATURE PARK After entering Bosnia and Herzegovina from the Croatian section of the Via Dinarica White Trail (or to hike the most attractive sections of the BiH trail), the most logical and accessible base on the western side of the trail is Blidinje Nature Park (Park prirode Blidinje, Masna Luka, Posušje; ✆ 039 718 514/5; **e** info@blidinje.net; **w** blidinje.net; ⊕ all year; no entrance fee). There are many access roads to the park, but it's best to stick to the three main roads via **Rakitno** northeast from **Posušje**, **Lipa** from **Tomislavgrad**, and due west from **Jablanica** via **Doljani**. No buses go through the park.

The park is set in long sweeping valleys. To the north and southeast are the 2,000m+ peaks of Vran and Čvrsnica. **Pločno** on Čvrsnica is the highest peak in Herzegovina at 2,228m. It is best to visit the park management building or the motel by the ski-lifts at **Risovac Ski Centre** (Masna Luka 29, Posušje; ✆ 039 718 514; **e** info@blidinje.biz; **w** blidinje. biz) for information about the park, its history and the **Franciscan monastery**, which is within the park and open to visitors.

Blidinje's vast valley is a popular summer destination for hikers and mountain bikers with the heart of the Via Dinarica trail covering both Vran and Cvrsnica Mountains. In the winter time, Via Dinarica is exciting for snow shoeing and tour skiing, but also for skiing at Risovac. It is one of the most remote nature parks in southeast Europe.

See pages 88–90 for more information on Blidinje Nature Park.

▲ Whitewater rafting on the Neretva River is a perfect day trip on the Via Dinarica (AB)

BORAČKO JEZERO (BORAČKO LAKE) Boračko jezero is a semi-glacial body of water set in the mountains in the central part of the Via Dinarica White Trail. It is an excellent place to rest after the long and challenging stages over Čvrsnica and Prenj mountains. The lake is open to the public for camping, swimming and barbecues, and a few of the locals have opened bed and breakfasts along the shores; there are also campsites. It costs 2KM per person to get into the lake area; the best spot is across the lake by the restaurant where you will find a great freshwater stream and plenty of shade. Swimming in the lake is highly recommended in the summer months.

Boračko jezero is also a good place to take a day's break and go white-water rafting on the Neretva River. About 5km away, the area between Konjic and the village of Glavetičevo is marked as campsites for the rafting companies that run trips down the Neretva Canyon. There is a good choice of accommodation facilities on the lake from apartments, B&Bs, and campsites to weekend home rentals, including **Boračko Lake Eco Village**, **Villa Sunce**, **Exo Log Cottage** (w exologistix.com/exologcottage; 270KM per cottage per night), **Boračko Lake Apartments** and **Herzegovina Lodges** (w hercegovina-lodges.com; from 50KM pp per night). See stages 31c and 32 on pages 113 and 114 for more information on where to stay and eat.

The rafting companies working in the area are: **Tudup Raft** (**w** tudupraft. com); **Hitko Rafting** (**w** hitkorafting.com); **Rafting Tours Salihamidžic** (**w** ambasadaneretva.com); and **Tajo-Raft Konjic** (**w** tajoraft.com).

For more information on the area around Boračko jezero, see pages 112–14.

UMOLJANI The natural beauty of Umoljani's surroundings is among the most striking in the area. The south side is a typical karst landscape that is dry and rather barren; the north side is lush with thick forest and green pastures and is ideal for hiking, walking or a picnic. The tombstones of ancient settlers can be found scattered around the village, with many medieval tombstones perched on high ridges.

The seven reconstructed old watermills on the left-hand (south) side on the approach to Umoljani are a great place to visit on a hike.

There are several *pansions* now in Umoljani, with the best being **Pansion Umoljani** (page 129). There are also two **restaurants** in the village: **Studeno vrelo** (page 128), situated in a log cabin close to the centre of the village and also offering very good accommodation; and **Koliba** (page 129), just past the main graveyard. Both offer magnificent views and excellent food. See stage 34 on pages 128–9 for more information on where to stay and eat.

There is no public transport going to Umoljani. By car, it is a little over an hour's drive from Sarajevo.

▼ The serpentine creek of Studeni potok near the village of Umoljani (b/S)

SUTJESKA NATIONAL PARK The main trailhead for the Via Dinarica White Trail, the 17,500ha Sutjeska National Park (Tjentište; ✆058 233 200; w npsutjeska.info) is rich both in wildlife and in mountain scenery, being the location of a number of the country's highest peaks. Maglić (2,386m), Bosnia and Herzegovina's highest summit, is on the Montenegrin border, and provides a demanding ascent. Guides can be hired, and there are now good maps detailing the many marked paths within the park. Accommodation in the mountains can be found on both the Maglić side (east) at the Prijevor katun huts run by the park, and in three mountain huts on the Zelengora side (west). The main hotel, Hotel Mladost (page 151), is in the Tjentište Valley near the main entrance to the park. The best restaurant in the area is **Restoran Tentorium** (Tjentište bb; m 065 414 465; mains 8–15KM). Located in the Tjentište Valley, just north of the park boundary, it serves an impressive selection of international and national dishes. Located next to the Hotel Mladost, there is a lovely shop called **Bio Špajz** (Bio Pantry), selling original, handmade souvenirs and organic and healthy local foods and drinks.

At **Tjentište**, the park's main settlement, there is a pair of fractal-wall monoliths built in remembrance of the Battle of Sutjeska, which took place during World War II and was one of the key battles fought by the Partisans in defending the free territories. The sheer enormity of the memorial makes it worth a look. Only 30 minutes southeast from Tjentište is the scenic-view area of **Perućica Primeval Forest**. The road is now well marked and halfway up the mountain there is a small ranger station, where you need to pay 5KM per person to enter the Perućica area of the park. There are information boards in English. Don't miss the 10-minute walk out to the ridge, which gives an utterly amazing view.

To reach Sutjeska, travelling from Sarajevo, take the Trnovo road almost to Foča before turning right (roads are marked) for the Trebinje–Dubrovnik road. At the turning, expect the road to become a bit narrower as you climb; the curvy bends barely give you enough room to stay on your side of the continuous road marking. Once you reach the top of the mountain (you'll know when you're there!) the massive faces of Zelengora and Maglić dominate the view. It's all downhill from there.

For more information on the park and its attractions, see pages 148–51.

▲ Maglić is Bosnia and Herzegovina's highest peak at 2,386m (SV/D)

▼ European brown bears are abundant in Perućica forest, one of the last primeval forests remaining in Europe (AB)

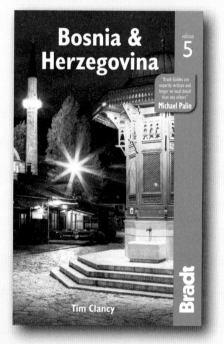

Part Two

WHITE TRAIL STAGES IN BOSNIA AND HERZEGOVINA

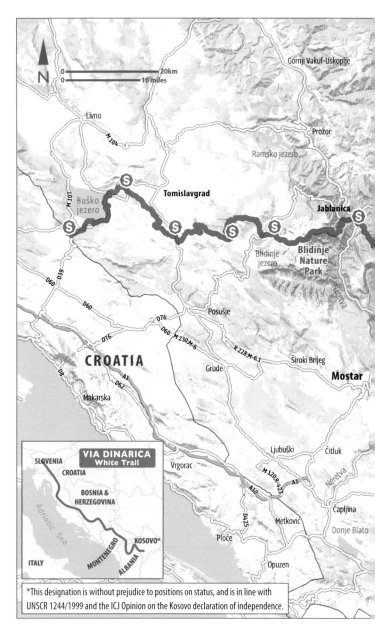

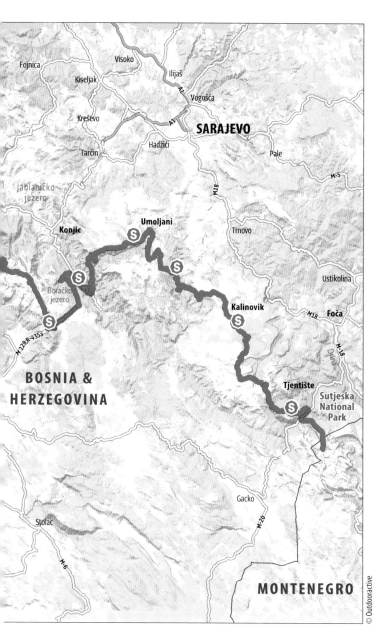

© Outdooractive

The Via Dinarica White Trail in Bosnia and Herzegovina starts in rural west Bosnia near the border with Croatia. This first stage of the Via Dinarica follows the pilgrim route dedicated to Our Lady of Sinj. The highlights on this first stage are the lovely vistas of Buško jezero (Buško Lake), several archaeological spots and the Grabovica Eco-Village. A large portion of this stage contains road walking so biking can be a practical alternative as well as the possibilities for kayaking and canoeing across the lake.

Start Border point Prisika (754m)
Coordinates ⊕ Geogr 43.606624 N 16.976123 E/UTM 33T 659478 4830080
Finish Mali Gradac – viewpoint (Privala: 993m) on Buško jezero
Difficulty easy
Distance 24.1km
Duration 10hrs
Ascent 570m
Descent 299m

🚶 **THE ROUTE** Several parts of this stage are on gravel or paved roads. From the border crossing with Croatia at **Prisika** head southeast to meet the road, then turn left (northeast) to Gornja Prisika, via Vrtline, where the route veers left and takes you to Kazaginac village. From Kazaginac, head north towards **Buško jezero** (Buško Lake) and **Marinovac Beach**, turn right (south) to rejoin the road before turning left (east) towards Bukova gora. Continue east along the road, with the option of either continuing east, or take the shortcut turning left (north) to **Carmel of Saint Elijah** and continue to Lonića kuća (clearly marked) in order to rejoin the road east. Continue along the road for just over 2km, turning northwest off the main road towards the lake. From there follow the minor road northwest towards 🏠 **Grabovica Eco-Village**, then continue west on the local paved road back to the main R417 road. It leads to the Karlov Han area, which is where you turn left (north) over the bridge to Prisoje village.

From the centre of Prisoje, go east to Brljevci village on the lake where 🏠 **Bošnjak household** is located and then continue on the dirt road uphill through the pine forest, past the rest area and viewpoint. The trail will join the main road below the 1,045m peak of **Mali Gradac**, where this stage ends.

WHAT TO SEE There aren't many places on the lake to visit. The ⌂ **Grabovica Eco-Village** offers a taste of the genuine natural beauty of the Buško jezero and the traditions of local hospitality. This is a higher-end facility, and certainly one of the best in the country. The Eco-Village is surrounded by mountains, making summer nights fresh and comfortable for sleeping during the hottest parts of the year. The tasteful combination of wood, stone and ceramic mosaic gives the apartments an archaic look, but all are equipped with modern amenities. This child-friendly establishment also has a small petting zoo with domestic and wild animals such as rabbits, deer, peacocks and hogs. However, the main animal attraction is the Equestrian Club, suitable for riders of all ages (one class with instructor costs 25KM). The facility can organise long-distance horseriding, mountain biking and hiking.

It can be simply a rest stop to overnight or used as a base to further explore the beautiful landscape of rural west Bosnia. The **Carmel of St Elijah Monastery and Spiritual Centre** is located just next to Buško jezero. The Catholic Church has a large presence in this part of the country, with St Elijah being one of the more accessible ecclesiastical buildings. There are a number of **caves** around the village of Prisoje, including the **Ričina Spring cave** some 3km east of the trail, just beyond Vrilo.

WHERE TO STAY AND EAT

⌂ **Grabovica Eco-Village** (40 beds; Grabovica bb, Prisoje; ☏ 034 366 851, 034 366 020; e info@ecoselgrabovica.com; w ecoselograbovica.com/en; 120–150KM B&B) This is an attractive lakeside village where you can taste some delicious local homemade eco-food

▼ Stage 26 takes walkers over the bridge to Prisoje village (B/S)

▲ Sunset over Buško Lake, one of the largest artificial lakes in Europe (OL)

inspired by rich regional traditions, such as *meze* with smoked meat, cheese, bread & beignets, roasted veal & lamb *ispod saca*, a variety of grilled dishes, & many soups & stews. Family friendly. It has some of the better accommodation in the wider area with clean, spacious rooms in rustic style, and it is advisable to book in advance. Open year-round.

🏠 **Bošnjak household** (10 beds; Prisoje bb, Prisoje; **m** 063 907 110; 20KM pp per night; breakfast 10KM) Bošnjak household is located in Prisoje, 18km from Tomislavgrad by road, & approximately 12km from Ponor (Šuica River sinkholes) via Grabovička Mountain by trail. It is beneath Tušnica Mountain & close to Buško jezero. The household offers accommodation for tourists & hikers visiting Buško jezero & the caves around Prisoje village.

🏠 **Tušnica Mountain House** (15 beds; Prisoje bb, Tomislavgrad; **m** 063 331 972; 20KM pp per night) This house, located 1km from the trail, serves as a gathering point for annual speleological meetings, & offers accommodation to tourists & hikers visiting Buško jezero & the caves around the village of Prisoje. It is still in modest condition, so we advise you to bring your own food & sleeping bag. There is also a camp area. Breakfast not served. Open on demand.

FURTHER PRACTICALITIES As the border crossing point at Vaganj (the pass between Troglav and Kamešnica) is just for locals and hence not an international border point, the last stage of the Croatian and first stage of the Bosnian Via Dinarica follows a pilgrim's trail: the Our Lady of Sinj Route. It is not possible to enter BiH from Croatia through the mountain crossing. All through-hikers must go to the official international border crossing at Prisika. This border crossing point will likely remain as the route of the main White Trail until such time as BiH joins the EU and Schengen treaty, or until Vaganj becomes the international border crossing point.

Other than a taxi or pre-organised trip with an operator or mountain club, no local transport is available.

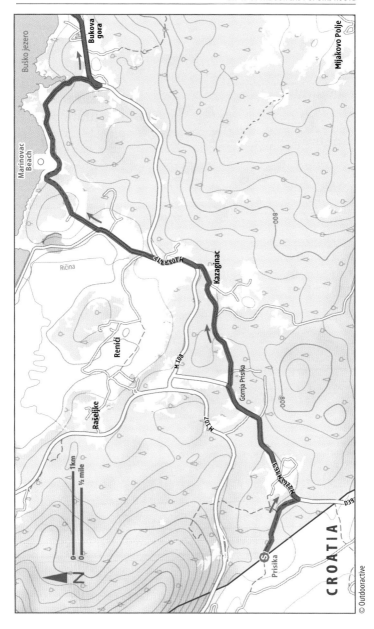

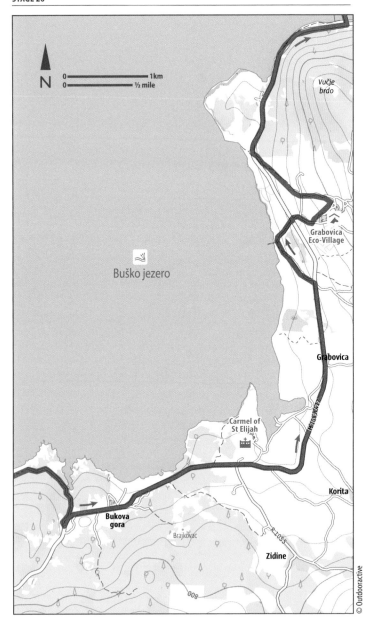

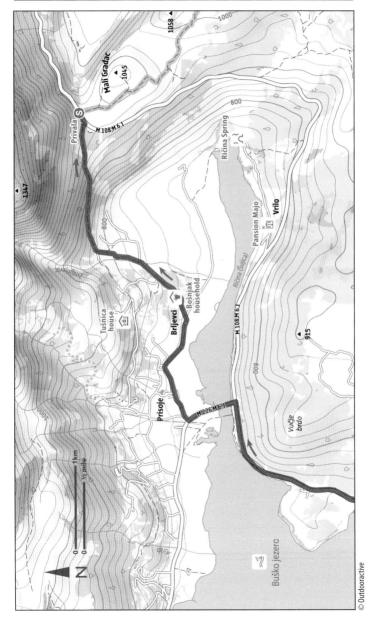

© Outdooractive

BH-W-02 VIA GRABOVIČKA PLANINA TO BUKOVICA AND DUVANJSKO POLJE

27

This is an easy 21km walk or mountain-bike ride with not many spectacular views, but an impressive glimpse into an amazing underground world. The area is dotted by many karst formations that have created a fascinating cave system, many of which can be explored only a short distance from the trail. Those include a cave that has the largest discovery of cave bear remnants in the country, the remains of ancient mammoths, archaeological sites, and the Šuica River sinkholes. From this long, open ridge, views over Buško jezero and Duvanjsko polje (Duvanjsko field) can be enjoyed almost throughout the entire stage.

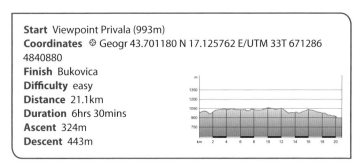

Start Viewpoint Privala (993m)
Coordinates ⊕ Geogr 43.701180 N 17.125762 E/UTM 33T 671286 4840880
Finish Bukovica
Difficulty easy
Distance 21.1km
Duration 6hrs 30mins
Ascent 324m
Descent 443m

🚶 THE ROUTE

The route largely maintains a southeasterly direction along a ridge road. This stage is best for biking or, if on foot, be prepared for a relatively flat walk on a gravel road. From the viewpoint at Privala below **Mali Gradac** mountain, follow the ridge road southeast with the peaks of Veliki Gradac (1,058m) rising to your left (north), and Gologlavo (984m) to the south. The access road (via 4x4 only) to the wind-turbine park connects several caves, pits and chasms. Continue southeast until you reach another road heading to your right (southwest). Take this short detour to visit the cave of **Mali Samograd**. Returning to the main trail to continue southeast will take in **Veliki Samograd** and ⊙ **Dahna Cave** below the route. Leaving Dahna Cave, after a further 1km you will cross the highest point of the stage, at 1,064m.

The route continues southeast for a short distance, then bears southwest to the village of Gornji Brišnik, where there is the **Monument of the rebel Mijat Tomić**. Leave the village heading initially south, then southeast for approximately 5.5km until a sharp change of direction northward brings you to the ⊙ **Bukovica Great Cathedral Cave**. From here, continue southeast to the main road.

▲ Stage 27 is a cavers' paradise as it is part of the world's largest karst field (MS)

Although this is one of the easier stages of the trail, there are no places to stay, or eat, available along the route until reaching the end point near Bukovica, so a tent and sufficient provisions may need to be carried.

WHAT TO SEE Again, it isn't the hike that is the most attractive part of this stage but rather what's hiding underground. **Surdup** is a sinkhole located on the path between the villages of Drmića Staje and Kovači. **Kovači Sinkhole** represents one of the most important speleological objects in the Tomislavgrad area. The entrance is located in Kovači village at 848m, just beneath Grabovička Mountain; its exit is on the eastern shore of Buško jezero. **Mali Samograd** is a deep cave that has an enormous vertical drop at the beginning, and is linked with a large sinkhole called Arnautovac. The length of the main channel of the cave is 135m, while the side channels are over 250m long. The depth of the pit is 150m. **Veliki Samograd** is a huge oval sinkhole cave that is about 190m long and 40–60m deep.

> **KARST**
>
> The limestone karst fields of Bosnia and Herzegovina are the largest in the world, creating amazing water sources and underground aquifer systems and caves.

Listvača is one of the most beautiful caves in the Duvno area, and is used by shepherds as a shelter from extreme weather. The total length of the cave is 103m, and is characterised by a surreal atmosphere of calcite carvings. **Dahna Cave** has a small entrance hidden in a hornbeam tree forest, under a rock covered with moss. Beyond the entrance space, there is a larger hall 20m long, 6–7m wide and 1–4m high, but beyond that is a massive 720m-long channel and then a 60m-long channel, where pottery artefacts from the Roman period were found. **Bukovica Great Cathedral Cave** has a high entrance chamber in which a powerful stream bursts from a very narrow hole. This stream once served as a driving mechanism for a millstone, which local people used to grind grains. Because of its natural ambience it also served as an altar in Ottoman times.

WHERE TO STAY AND EAT

Lovre (Bukovica bb, Tomislavgrad; ☏ 034 316 100, **m** 063 330 366; **w** lovre-tg.com; 20KM pp per night; breakfast 10KM) Located 1km north of Bukovica, on the Tomislavgrad–Posušje section of the main M15 road. Open year-round.

Pizzeria Pećina (Bukovica bb, Tomislavgrad; ☏ 034 316 310; 6–16KM per meal) Located close to 2 beautiful unexplored caves. Open year-round.

FURTHER PRACTICALITIES For further information on the caves, contact Naša baština (**m** 063 332 822; **e** miro.sumanovic@tel.net. ba; **f** nasa.bastina.tg), or the local caving club **Mijatovi Dvori** (Mijat's Castles) (**m** 063 331 972).

There is no local transport covering this stage of the route other than taxis or a pre-organised trip with an operator or mountain club.

▼ The entrance to the Cathedral Cave near Tomislavgrad (MS)

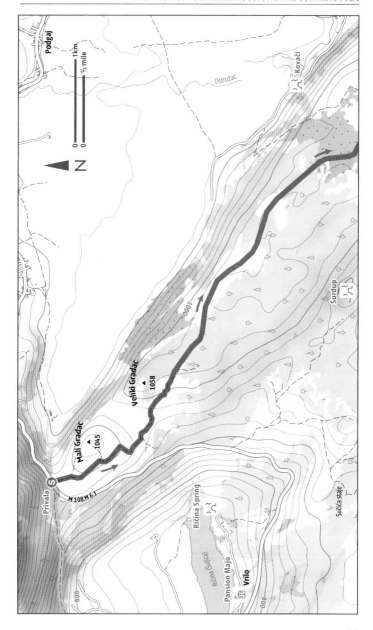

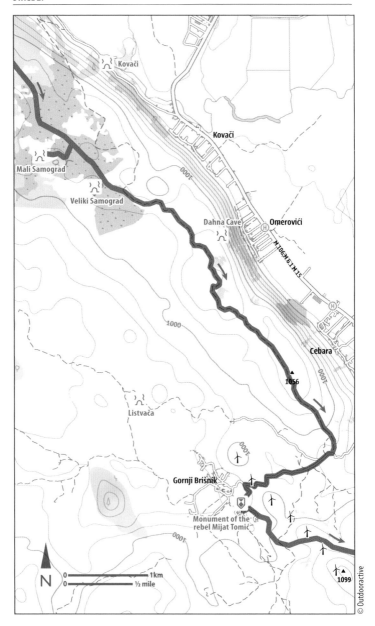

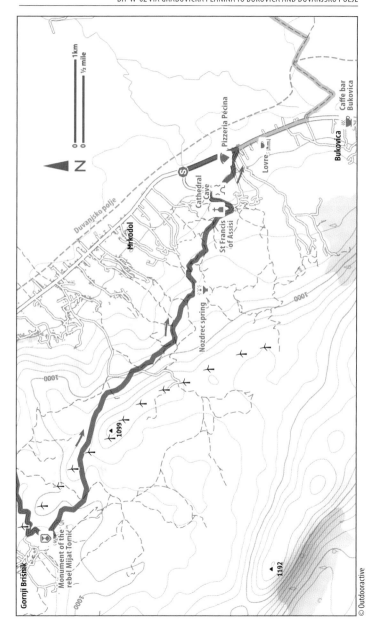

© Outdooractive

28 BH-W-03 LIB AND SVINJAR

This trail connects Duvanjsko polje and Blidinje Nature Park. Although it is less known as a hiking area, there are great views of Duvanjsko polje, Vran and Čvrsnica mountains. This is where the trail enters the higher mountain areas of the Via Dinarica White Trail in Bosnia and Herzegovina.

In the first section of this stage, the trail crosses Duvanjsko polje and comes to the village of Omolje. From Omolje it climbs up to Orlov kuk (Vrlokuk) and Lib Mountain where it continues towards its north ridge, shared with Mt Svinjar. From the summit of Mt Svinjar, the trail descends to Svinjača's end on the road to Blidinje. The second section of this stage continues on the opposite side of the road, towards Vran Mountain and ends in the shepherd settlement called Omrčenica.

Start Bukovica, on the Tomislavgrad–Mostar road (881m)
Coordinates ⊕ Geogr 43.616180 N 17.265105 E/UTM 33T 682771 4831737
Finish Omrčenica
Difficulty moderate
Distance 28.8km
Duration 7hrs
Ascent 1,195m
Descent 700m

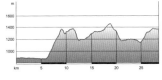

🚶 **THE ROUTE** Starting from Bukovica village, follow the road southeast towards Posušje town and look for a sign and road leading to the **Duvanjsko polje**. After 2km, turn left (northeast) on to a less developed road and follow it to the end, then cross the bridge after the graveyard. From this point, cross the asphalt road in Omolje village, follow the street to the end and turn right (east) after the markings. The trail veers east, then northeast into a small forest where it eventually bends left (northwest), with two permanent mountain springs to your right (east), towards Orlov kuk summit. At the trail crossing near the summit, turn right (east) towards Mt Svinjar (in the direction of Čvrsnica Mountain), as the other trail will descend to Borčane and the Grla Valley. After crossing an interesting valley with steep walls, the trail heads towards the north ridge and follows it to Svinjar peak (1,269m), and then descends eastwards to **Svinjača** to the R419a road.

The trail continues in the pine forests on the southern slopes of Vran Mountain and initially heads north, passing by a few private properties and weekend homes, some of which are available for rent or as campsites. Follow the forest track for approximately 3.5km to the first crossing, where you should turn right (north) (direction **Vesine staje, Omar**). On exiting the forest, you will reach an open meadow in Omar. From Omar, turn right (northwest) to the first track from the main road and continue past the house on the right. When you reach the road again after a further 0.5km, bear right (east) and then turn off the road uphill to the left until you reach another open area, **Omrčenica**, where the ascent to Mali Vran begins.

There are no places to eat along the back half of this stage, so be sure to pack sufficient food supplies. There is accommodation available in Omrčenica in cottages or weekend huts. This can be arranged with the locals from Omolje or Mandino villages. All of the contact information for these facilities can be found on **w** viadinarica.com. As these are not permanently inhabited households, it is best to call ahead to make reservations.

WHAT TO SEE St Anthony's Chapel was built in the 1920s to honour St Anthony, the saint of lost things, in gratitude that her two sons had returned unharmed from World War I. The chapel is set in a mountain

▼ Steep limestone rock faces in the Grla Valley (MS)

▲ Winter hiking on stage 28 (MS)

field called Svinjača, at the foot of Vran Mountain. It is worth mentioning that the north ridge of Lib leads to an ancient Iliryan capital that was called **Deliminium**. There is not much to see on the spot, but it is good to know that once upon a time it was a main centre of the Dalmatian tribes.

WHERE TO STAY AND EAT
Holiday house at Vran mountain (6 beds; Brišnik bb; Tomislavgrad; **m** 063 330 626; **e** sarac.mirko@tel.net.ba; open on demand) Simply furnished house, located 2km north of Omrčenica.

FURTHER PRACTICALITIES There are **two permanent springs** along this route, however, they have been known to go dry in the summer months. Be sure to carry enough water with you for this stage. Contact the local club Orlova Stina Mountain Club (Mijata Tomića bb; **m** 063 330 097; **e** ante.vukadin@tel.net.ba) from Tomislavgrad, especially if you plan to continue your journey over Vran Mountain or if you need suggestions for accommodation.

If you're not planning to walk the adjoining stages of the route, you'll need to make your own way there as there is no local public transport.

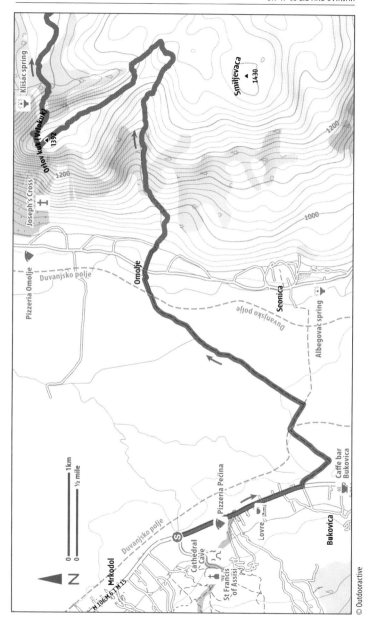

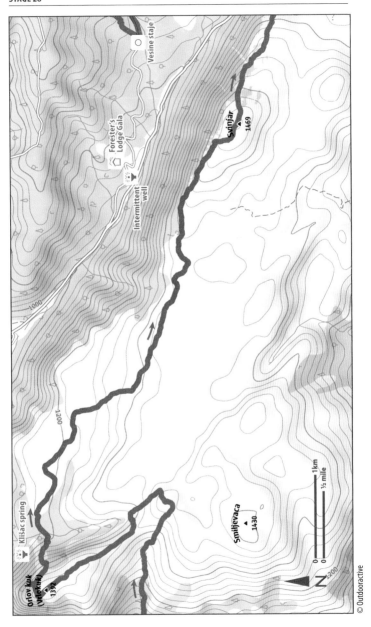

© Outdooractive

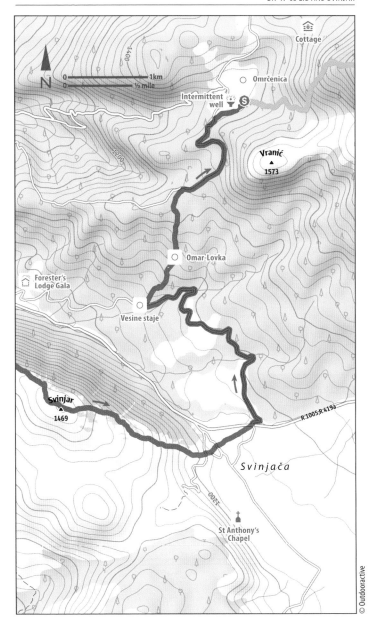

Stage 29 leads into the vast valley where the Blidinje Nature Park is located. This area is known for good hiking with great views on Čvrsnica Mountain and Blidinje jezero (Blidinje Lake) to the east, Ljubuša and Duvanjsko polje to the west, and Raduša Mountain to the northwest. The trail crosses the mountain ridge from Mali Vran to Vran and descends to Blidinje Lake where a mountain hut is located or, alternatively, to Hajdučke Vrleti mountain motel for a nice hot meal.

Start Omrčenica
Coordinates ⊕ Geogr 43.647511 N 17.418810 E/UTM 33T 695073 4835566
Finish Blidinje Lake Mountain Lodge
Difficulty moderate
Distance 11.3km
Duration 5hrs 15mins
Ascent 744m
Descent 930m

THE ROUTE From **Omrčenica**, the ascent to Mali Vran summit begins. The climb is not long, but is rather steep.

At the ridge beneath **Mali Vran**, turn right (east) towards the summit at 1,961m (the other trail descends down towards a small weekend settlement). From here, with splendid views of Blidinje Lake and Čvrsnica Mountain, follow the markings all the way to the summit of **Vran** (2,020m). Once at the peak of Vran, turn right (south) and descend over steep terrain to the local road that will bring you to the 🏠 **Blidinje Lake Mountain Lodge** on the shore of the lake.

You can alternatively continue towards Veliki (Great) Vran summit for another 2 hours, and descend to Hajdučke Vrleti mountain hotel, where you can have a great hot meal or overnight there.

WHAT TO SEE ◉ **Blidinje Nature Park** is a visually stunning environment. The impressive natural endowments of the park include the highest summits of Vran Mountain, including Veliki Vran at 2,074m, and Vran, which has an altitude of 2,020m. Additionally, the park has some interesting cultural heritage to explore, including Saint Elijah's Church and Masna Luka Monastery. **Masna Luka** is a Franciscan monastery located at an altitude of 1,200m. **Saint Elijah's Church** is an artistically decorated church of St Elias and also part of the monastery. Near the

The open and barren valley leading into the **Blidinje Nature Park** is a result of the past two ice ages. The melting glaciers from Čvrsnica created this massive valley between the **Čvrsnica** and **Vran mountains.** This runway for ice, water and debris did not, however, manage to stop a wide range of life forms from prospering here. To contrast some of the rocky and seemingly lifeless slopes are thick forests of pine, including the endemic white bark pine (*Pinus leucodermis*). Three types of wild thyme and dozens of wildflowers cover the valley and mountainsides in the spring and summer.

The 3–5km valley, situated at an elevation ranging from 1,150m to 1,300m, is dotted with the trademark *stećci* tombstones from medieval times. It is not clear how long human settlements have existed here, but research began when Blidinje received nature park status. Traces of Illyrian graves and Roman roads indicate that Blidinje has been settled for at least 2,500 years. For more information on Blidinje Nature Park, see page 61.

Hajdučke Vrleti motel in the middle of the valley there is a necropolis of stećci, part of the **UNESCO World Heritage Site**.

WHERE TO STAY AND EAT

Hajdučke Vrleti (50 beds; Blidinje bb, Tomislavgrad; 039 718 522; 40–70KM pp per night) Situated around 3km northeast of the Via Dinarica trail from Blidinje jezero, this is the largest hotel in the valley & is open all year round. The restaurant is quite popular & serves

▼ Blidinje Lake in Blidinje Nature Park (EO)

▲ St Elijah's Church and Franciscan Monastery in Masna Luka (OL)

many local specialities. The hotel facilities are basic but clean & reliable. Many hikers choose to overnight here.

🏠 **MTB Blidinje** (8 beds; Risovac bb; **m** 063 403 119; **e** mtb_blidinje@yahoo.com; **w** mtb-blidinje.net; 50KM pp per night) MTB specialises in biking trips in & around Blidinje Nature Park. They also have a nice traditional restaurant near the ski-lifts at the **Risovac Ski Centre** nearby, as well as having apartments & 8 comfortable rooms on offer at the Boarding House Vilinac. They are a highly professional organisation with proper equipment, good guides, & excellent knowledge of the area. MTB & the Ski Centre are 6.5km from the trail & there is no transport within the valley to move around unless earlier arranged with MTB or other service providers.

🏠 **Blidinje Lake Mountain Lodge** (34 beds; Blidinje bb, Blidinje; **m** 063 330 097; 20KM pp per night) The lodge is located on the western shore of Blidinje jezero, by the Tomislavgrad–Posušje–Blidinje–Jablanica road. There are indoor bathrooms & showers. It is accessible by vehicle & has space for parking. They do not offer food, but Hajdučke Vrleti restaurant is 3km northeast from the lodge on the same main road. The mountain lodge is open on demand.

FURTHER PRACTICALITIES There are four **intermittent wells** and three **natural springs** along this route. Also, along this route are the crossroads of Vesine Staje and Omar-Lokva.

Other than a taxi or pre-organised trip with an operator or mountain club, no local transport is available.

Administration building – Nature Park Blidinje (📞039 718 515; **e** zdravkokutle@gmail.com; **w** blidinje.net; **w** pp-blidinje.com). They do not currently provide any service to visitors.

This is a great hike over Čvrsnica, the highest mountain in Herzegovina. It follows the Vilinac ridge over Drinjača summit and Plasa plateau, and descends to the town of Jablanica in the Neretva River Valley.

Trail runners and light and fit hikers can complete this stage in one long day. However, it is nice to take your time and fully enjoy the mountain over two or even three days of hiking. The nights can be spent in Vilinac or Plasa mountain huts. The viewpoint close by Vilinac hut is truly spectacular.

Start Blidinje Lake Mountain Lodge
Coordinates ⊕ Geogr 43.619447 N 17.503624 E/UTM 33T 702007 4832652
Finish Jablanica
Difficulty moderate
Distance 35.5km
Duration 14hrs 45mins
Ascent 1,329m
Descent 2,343m

THE ROUTE This long stage starts from the Blidinje Lake Mountain Lodge. All bottles should be filled here, as the rest of the hike does not have consistent water supplies.

Follow the trail marking across the field heading northeast towards the forested gorge at the base of the Čvrsnica Mountain. The trail will eventually join the forest road, continue to follow it to the end. At this point one can see a few houses. Soon after the end of the road, the trail continues to the trail crossing. Here, at the signpost you will continue right (southeast).

The trail ascends following an old shepherd's route all the way to the pass. A few kilometres after the pass, in a markedly green valley, there is a less obvious trail splitting to the left (north), beneath the peak of Juneći kuk (1,911m). Take this trail which head towards Mali Vilinac (1,996m) in the distance. On the next trail crossing you will continue straight (north). These junctions are all marked. In the vicinity of Mali Vilinac the trail dips down towards the beginning of the Veliki Vilinac ridge.

Follow the ridge of Veliki Vilinac southeast to Prigon saddle. The 🏠 **Vilinac Mountain Lodge** hut is 200m below to the south of the trail on the right. It is a perfect spot to rest and overnight. If you intend to carry on towards Plasa, the trail actually continues left, the next crossing is just 200m ahead; from there, go right (east), passing **Crvenjak jezero** (Crvenjak Lake) *en route*. At **Hajdučka vrata** (Rebel's Gate), continue straight up to **Drinjača** summit (2,038m) and do not descend towards the Diva

Grabovica Valley. Continuing east, after a further 3km, the trail swings to the southwest, leading to the 🏠 **Plasa hut**. At Plasa hut head east, then north, pass a number of water sources (one is clearly marked) and descend a series of switchbacks. The trail will bring you to a 4x4 road. Follow this road and disregard the less-used branches off it. If in doubt, turn left. There will be one junction, and there you should turn left. The water source on the descending way is marked by a sign. The road will pass by Jablanica's landfill (not a nice place after Cvrsnica, but only option at the moment) and soon you will reach the asphalt road, where you turn right for a further 2km to arrive in Jablanica town. This part of the trail isn't as attractive as the hike over the mountain. There are plans to redirect the trail directly into Jablanica town that will eliminate this section.

There will be a large curve as the main road veers left (northeast). Cross this road and go straight on, then right (south) at the T-crossing. Follow the road to the cemetery and look for the footpath in the bushes and trees opposite, on the left side. Follow this path to go down the stairs to Jablanica's main road. The next stage of the trail begins on the other side of the 👁 **Neretva River**, at the **crossroads**, after the tunnel.

WHAT TO SEE Čvrsnica is one of the most beautiful mountains in Bosnia and Herzegovina, and definitely one of the highlights of the Via Dinarica

👁 The **Neretva River** has its beginnings south of Zelengora Mountain in Sutjeska National Park in the Borač region near the border with Montenegro, travelling some 230km into the Adriatic Sea at Ploče in neighbouring Croatia. In its upper section, the river forces its way between the massifs of the Visočica and the Bjelašnica mountains in the north, and between the massifs of the Crvanj and the Prenj mountains in the south. It flows through numerous canyons and a smaller number of fertile valleys.

Unlike the other Bosnian rivers, the Neretva River does not succeed in forcing its way further north. Passing to the north of the Prenj massif, the river turns south somewhere near the mouth of the Rama tributary. It then forces its way through the canyons between the Prenj and Čvrsnica mountains, until it reaches the Mostar Valley, where it loses the character of a rapid mountain river. This emerald beauty is in grave danger. Bosnia and Herzegovina's political elite have often been accused of being ecologically illiterate – and the Neretva is unfortunately suffering because of it. Although the Upper Neretva River is a vast resource of fresh and potable water, the energy lobbies are pushing to build several hydro-electric dams that would forever ruin its unique characteristics and wildlife. Environmental groups have been met with threats and obstruction, but continue to fight to preserve one of Europe's richest ecosystems.

through pristine mountain wilderness. Being only 9.5km from Jablanica town, it is also very accessible. The first part of the stage goes through young munika (*Pinus heldreichii* – endemic species of pine) forest and some beech at the end of the forest belt. Highland landscapes are dominated by Alpine scrub and carpets of dwarf-pines (*Pinus mugo*). It hosts the most elevated mountain lodge along the entire Via Dinarica: the 🏠 **Vilinac Mountain Lodge** located at 1,964m, as well as a couple of small lakes and the glorious rock eye of **Hajdučka vrata** (Rebel's Gate). This section of the Via Dinarica offers great views of Vran Mountain, **Pločno summit**, Pešti brda, Diva Grabovica Valley and Doljanka Valley.

The town of Jablanica is of course the main place to resupply, but also to visit sites such as the famous **Battle for the Wounded on Neretva River Museum** (☎036 752 705, **m** 061 175 317; **w** muzej-jablanica.com), and the **Broken bridge on the Neretva River**. For more information on Jablanica, see page 54.

🏠 **WHERE TO STAY AND EAT** In Jablanica, there are at least a half-dozen restaurants specialising in the famous local delicacy, lamb on the spit.

🏠 **Motel Hollywood** (5 rooms; Pere Bilića bb, Jablanica ☎ 036 752 863; 50KM). This motel is the only accommodation facility in Jablanica's town centre. It's a no-frills place that is close to the trail. The staff are helpful & friendly. The rooms are basic but have hot water & are all en suite. The bar below is definitely added value.

🏠 **Vilinac Mountain Lodge** (30 beds; Čvrsnica Mountain; **m** 061 043 241; **w** vilinac.ba; 12KM pp per night; breakfast 6KM) A modest lodge with 2 sources of drinking water in the

▼ Crvenjak jezero is about half way along Stage 30 (EO)

▲ The 'Rebel's Gate' is a naturally eroded rock formation on Čvrsnica Mountain (EO)

immediate vicinity & an outdoor toilet. Located at 1,961m below the eponymous peak Čvrsnica – Veliki Vilinac, with stunning views of Prenj mountain range. ⊕ Jun–Nov, remaining months on demand.

🏠 **Plasa Mountain Hut** (20 beds; Čvrsnica Mountain; m 061 387 925, 063 850 706; 12KM pp per night; breakfast 6KM) A small hut set in a remote area of Čvrsnica Mountain at 1,620m. Powered by solar panels, no running water available, but there is a wellspring a 5min walk from the hut. Organised mountain climbing tours on request. ⊕ Open during the summer, winter on demand.

✕ **Zdrava Voda** (Zdrava Voda bb, M-17; ✆ 036 753 151; w zdravavoda.co.ba; 20–30KM). This is the closest of the famous lamb-on-the-spit restaurants to Jablanica town centre. It is a very popular stopover for travellers going north & south & is almost always crowded. You can take away grilled lamb as well for the next stage of your trip as there won't be any more restaurants on stage 31.

✕ **Restoran Kovačević** (Donja Jablanica M-17 bb; ✆ 036 754 500; w www.restoran-kovacevic.ba; 20KM). This is one of the better lamb restaurants just outside of Jablanica on the M-17 road. Aside from superb lamb on the spit, the terraced dining area has spectacular views of the Neretva River & Prenj Mountain.

FURTHER PRACTICALITIES Water from a number of **wells and springs** can be found in only a few places, so note that you will need to refill at each of them. Most of the hiking is pleasant, with ascents not too steep and altitude losses not significant; nevertheless, it can be hot in windless summer days.

There is no local transport covering this stage of the route other than taxis or a pre-organised trip with an operator or mountain club.

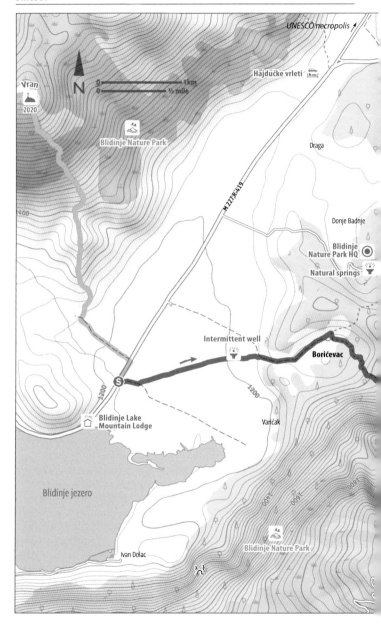

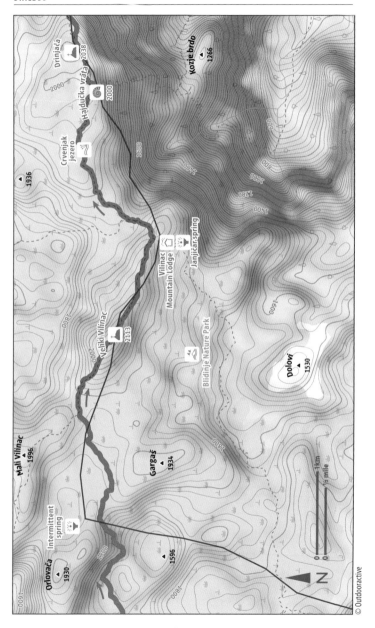

© Outdooractive

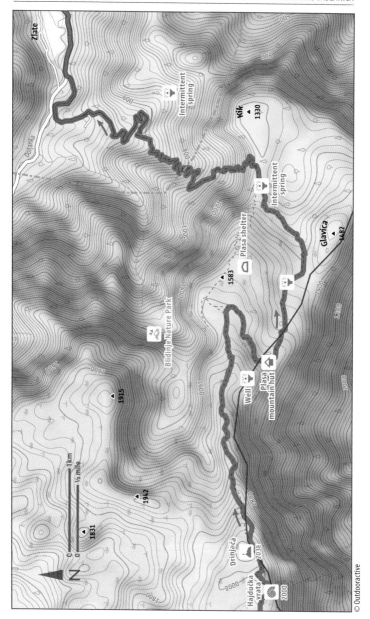

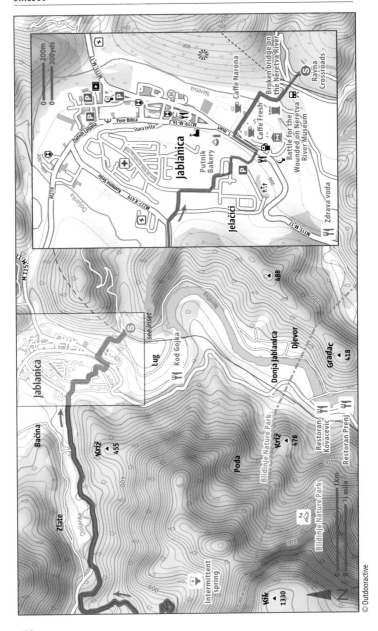

Hikers on the challenging
Prenj Mountain stage (KM)

🛡31 BH-W-06 PRENJ MOUNTAIN

This is an epic hike over one of the most attractive mountains in Bosnia and Herzegovina. Prenj is an adventure in itself including ascents to some of the highest peaks of the Via Dinarica White Trail and amazing karst scenery. Stage 31 is broken up into three sub-stages as the hike over Prenj is challenging and long.

Start Jablanica, after the bridge on the Neretva River (191m)
Coordinates ⊕ Geogr 43.652450 N 17.765087 E/UTM 33T 722982 4836988
Finish Rujište (1,053m)
Difficulty difficult
Distance 36.4km
Duration 16hrs 30mins
Ascent 2,823m
Descent 1,955m

🚶 THE ROUTE

Stage 31a This stage ranks among the steepest and hardest sections along the whole Via Dinarica trail. It is rather straightforward, however. Cross the bridge over the Neretva and walk through the tunnel to reach the trailhead at Ravna Crossroads on the left side of the road. Follow the marked trail over the hills for 3.5km, initially heading southeast then south at a permanent spring, all the way to Ravna. There are a couple of junctions with other smaller trails, so just make sure that you continue in a southward direction to remain on the marked trail. Cross the road in the village of Ravna and look for the trail signs passing by the local school and leading up (south) to the woods. Hike on the marked trail for several hours (around 6.5km) until you reach the mountain hut at 🏠 **Međuprenje**, situated next to the old 🏠 **Milanova koliba**, with Cetina Mountain (1,991m) above the hut. The latter stages of this particular section of the trail are more exposed and narrow in some places.

Stage 31b From the mountain huts at Međuprenje, continue up towards Greda Pass. Soon you will reach the junction close by remnants of the old shepherds' hut. Here you can take the trail going right (southwest) to the dwarf pine bush, but also the one to the east continuing over rocky slopes towards Greda Pass. The former is easier to walk on and eventually it will join the one from Greda. After some 20 minutes, you'll find a spring at the bottom of the scree slope to the right beneath a rock when descending towards Lučine. Past the newly built **shelter** in Lučine, continue east. At the next crossing towards Lupoglav summit, remain on the trail (left then straight, strictly adhering to the trail marking). Before the main crossing in Tisovica (you can see a sign pole from a distance), you'll join a trail going towards ⌂ **Vrutak hut** and **Zelena Glava summit** (2,108m); there, go right (southeast). Just below the hut in the forest, you will pass next to a mine-suspected area which is marked and blocked by logs. Just stay on the clearly visible trail.

Stage 31c The trail climbs up to the Podotiš area, with the peak of **Otiš** (2,097m) nearby, and close to its highest point there is a crossing where you should go right (west) for the trail climbing to Zelena Glava and Otiš peaks, returning the same way. If you don't want to climb Zelena Glava, continue south. Keep straight all the way for a further 6km, in a south to southwesterly direction, to ⌂ **Bijele Vode katun** (old shepherd's hut) and the ⌂ **Adnan Krilić Mountain Lodge** a short distance beyond. Continue straight down the trail through the beech forest, and then on to an old forestry road. After just over 2km in the woods you can turn to the left (south) over a small meadow, or remain on the road, as it will lead you to the same point. At the ruin look for the trail markings again, and follow them all the way to Rujište. When you reach the main road go left again (east), and that will lead you to Rujište.

WHAT TO SEE The trail crosses almost all of ◉ Prenj from west to south. This offers plenty of things to see and boasts some of the finest views and terrain on all of the Via Dinarica. The pass over the hill to the village of Ravna on an exposed ridge offers great views on **Cetina rock face** – more than 1,000m of pure limestone. To reach the **Lučine Valley** one crosses **Zakantar**, a huge karst plateau and a natural habitat of the endemic Prenj salamander (seen only during the night and rainy weather). Zakantar terminates above the amazing **Tisovica Valley**, which ends on the slopes of Prenj's highest peaks – Zelena glava. The summits of **Zelena glava** (altitude 2,155m) and **Otiš** (altitude 2,097m) are both challenging climbs. From **Bijele Vode**, or White Waters, the trail descends towards Rujište settlement and recreation area. **Rujište** is a popular destination for a day trip from Mostar. There you will find two other mountain lodges, a hotel

◉ **Prenj**, with its sharp, tooth-like peaks, is part of a chain of mountains known as the Herzegovina Himalayas. The lowlands, by contrast, are very accessible and offer scenic drives. The area is known for its numerous endemic species of wildflowers only found in this region of the world. Honey and trout are also trademarks of this region.

Looking across the Tisovica
Valley to the peaks of Prenj (AB)

and a small ski centre. From here you can get a lift to Mostar by calling a taxi or continue the hike on a mountain road towards Boračko jezero (Boračko Lake).

 WHERE TO STAY AND EAT
Stage 31a
🏠 **Međuprenje mountain hut** (25 people capacity; Prenj Mountain; m 061 499 320; 10KM pp per night; breakfast 4KM) A newly built hut with solar panels & an outdoor toilet. Full-board optional, call in advance.

🏠 **Milanova koliba** (10 people capacity; Prenj Mountain; m 062 884 520) Located at 1,513m, this hut serves as a shelter from extreme weather conditions. You need to have your own sleeping bag & food. Open year-round.

Stage 31b
🏠 **Vrutak mountain hut** (10 beds; Prenj Mountain; m 061 918 891; 10KM pp per night). A charming hut located at 1,606m in one of the most attractive locations on Prenj Mountain, beneath the summits of Otiš & Zelena Glava. It has no electricity, has an outdoor toilet, & the nearest water source is about a 20min walk away. Open on demand.

Stage 31c
🏠 **Snježna kuća Motel** (36 beds; Park Prirode Rujište bb; ☎ 036 502 500; w snjeznakuca. info; 40KM pp B&B) The motel is surrounded by beautiful pine forests. Offers mountain biking, skiing & snowboarding. Open year-round.

🏠 **Adnan Krilić Mountain Lodge** (30 beds; Bijele Vode Valley; m 061 528 562; 20KM pp per night; breakfast 4KM) It is located at 1,450m, uses solar panels, & there is a water spring 150m from the lodge. An ideal base camp for exploring the Prenj peaks. Full board optional, call in advance. Open on demand.

🏠 **Rujište Mountain Lodge** (42 beds; Rujište bb; m 061 528 562; 20KM pp per night; breakfast 4KM) The lodge is located on the saddle of Prenj & Velež mountains, 25km from Mostar, at 1,050m. It is surrounded by a lush green forest of mainly endemic pine trees that have a multitude of medicinal qualities. It has public electricity access & cold & hot running water. For full board options, call in advance. Open year-round.

🏠 **Bijele Vode shelter** (4 beds; Bijele Vode Valley; m 061 528 562) A small shelter from the extreme weather conditions. Open year-round.

FURTHER PRACTICALITIES Along this route are very few **natural springs and wells**. In the heat of the summer (July–August) water can be an issue on the trail. Be sure to bring enough to last at least a day's hiking (2l minimum).

A lift to Mostar is only possible by calling a taxi. There is no transport in this area. It can be arranged through the hotel reception of Snježna kuća.

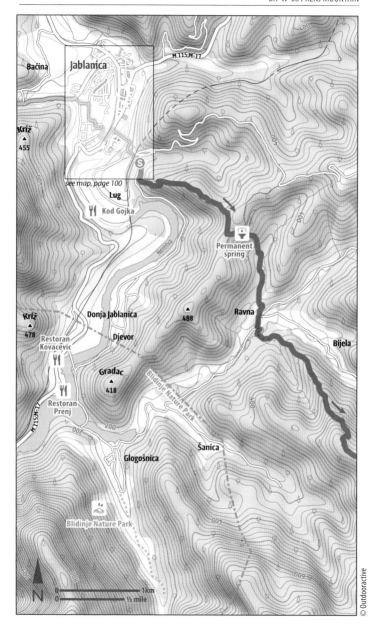

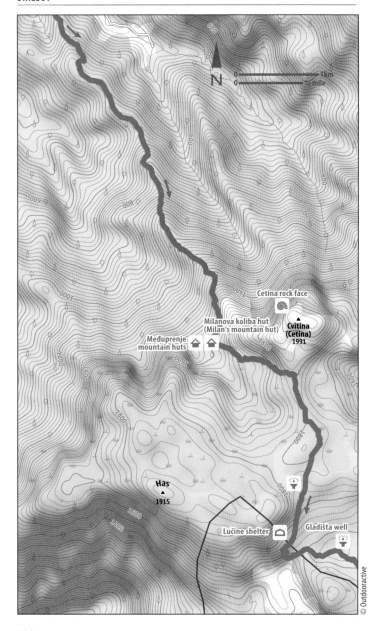

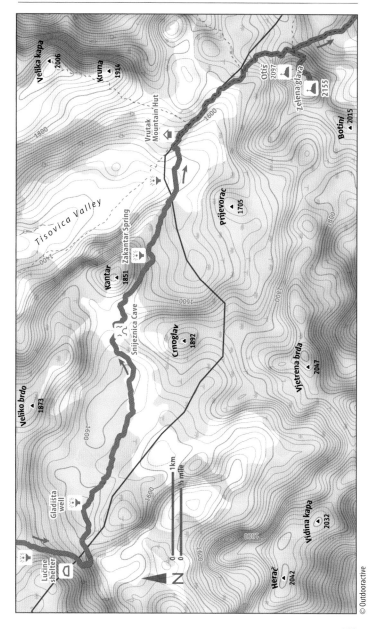

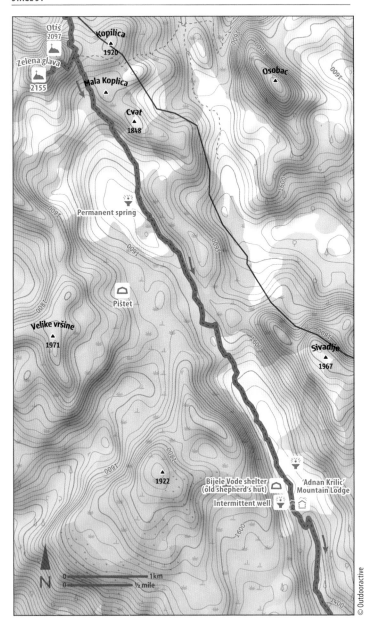

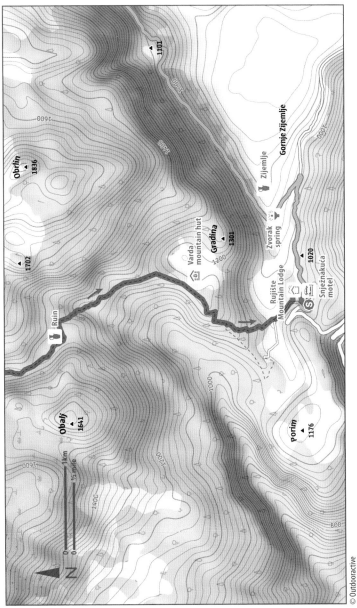

© Outdooractive

This stage doubles as a mountain bike and hiking trail that goes from Rujište to Boračko jezero (Boračko Lake). It passes by two interesting necropolises of Bosnian medieval tombstones (stećci) and the ruin of Šantića Villa.

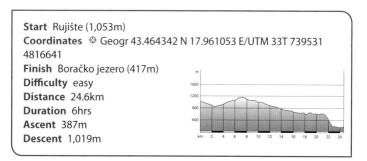

Start Rujište (1,053m)
Coordinates ⊕ Geogr 43.464342 N 17.961053 E/UTM 33T 739531 4816641
Finish Boračko jezero (417m)
Difficulty easy
Distance 24.6km
Duration 6hrs
Ascent 387m
Descent 1,019m

🕱 **THE ROUTE** The trail follows the road going from Rujište to Boračko jezero, along the easternmost slopes of Prenj Mountain. Despite the trail's proximity to this great mountain, there are no views of Prenj landscapes, however, there are impressive views of Crvanj Mountain and Boračko jezero.

From Rujište settlement, head left (east) to begin a long section of road walking. The road leads to Borci village, making a number of directional changes and passing a couple of water sources and two necropolises of medieval tombstones *en route*. This makes for fairly level walking, with little height gain or loss. At the road junction, just beyond the second necropolis, Velika poljana, continue to head northwest on the main road. At the far end of Bahtijevica, where the trail turns to the west, there is a nice **viewpoint on Mount Visočica**, and canyons of the Neretva and Rakitnica rivers. The next portion of the Via Dinarica trail is actually visible from this viewpoint.

The road and the trail splits at the junction not far from this viewpoint. One is a shorter way directly to Boračko jezero via the village of Kula, but at the junction to Kula, continue straight on towards the Boračka Draga and Borašnica Mountain, and at the next junction to Crno polje (Prenj), turn right (northeast). Just before the cemetery at Borci, there is a trail going right down, but to stay on the Via Dinarica, continue a couple of hundred metres more and then turn southwest to the ruins of **Šantića Villa**. The trail continues on the other side of the villa's garden, behind the **grave of Lazara Drljače**. Passing close to a couple more water sources, the trail continues southeast for around 2km into the valley of Boračko jezero. Once down in the lake's valley, follow the road on the left (north) side of the lake, though following the southern shore is also an option as you would then pass by the main beach of Boračko Lake. The stage ends on the shore of Boračko jezero at the administration centre. At the lake there is a shop, restaurants and guesthouses. For more information on Boračko jezero, see pages 62–3.

Although this is one of the trail's easier days, there is no accommodation or eating places available along the route until reaching the end point at Boračko jezero, so a tent (and food) may need to be carried.

WHAT TO SEE The trail passes by two necropolises of medieval tombstones called *stećci*: one below the junction to Nevesinje and another in the Bahtijevica area. The second, at **Velika poljana** is a national monument, covering over 1,000m^2 and features 47 tombstones, 13 of which are richly decorated with some particularly interesting carvings.

At Borci, there is **Šantića Villa**. Built in Borci in 1902, this villa was once the residence of the famous poet Aleksa Šantić when he was expelled from Mostar by the Austrian authorities in 1913 for publishing patriotic poems.

WHERE TO STAY AND EAT

Boračko Lake Apartments (4 rooms & 4 apts; Boračko jezero; **m** 062 115 015; **e** info@ borackojezero.com; **w** borackojezero.com; 54KM pp per night; breakfast 4KM) The most luxurious accommodation on the lake. Just 100m from Prenj Beach, all rooms & apartments are decorated in modern style in light colours & outfitted with chic wooden furniture. Each unit has a TV, & most importantly, a balcony with a lake view. Prices are up to 20% lower in the winter. Its restaurant serves excellent trout. Rafting tours upon request. Open May–Oct.

Herzegovina Lodges (30 beds; Boračko jezero bb; **☏** 036 288 236; **w** hercegovina- lodges.com; 30–80KM pp per night; breakfast 10–15KM, group discounts available) Traditional, Bosnian-style lodges that offer modern comforts. They organise rafting, mushroom & medicinal herb-picking tours, & a Herzegovina wine route visit. Call in advance to arrange any of the tours. Open Apr–Dec; other months on demand only.

Villa Sunce (45 beds; Boračko jezero; **m** 062 111 577; **w** vila-sunce.com; 28–36KM pp B&B) Located 250m from the beach, just above the Šthe ab River, with a spectacular view of the Prenj massif rock cliffs from the main outside sitting area. The villa is suitable for group tours. The English-speaking staff are exceptionally friendly & open to conversing with guests while preparing food & drink in the outside dining area. They can organise single-day trips of your liking, whether it be rafting, hiking, fishing or cycling. The rooms are basic but quite comfortable, & are all en suite. The kitchen & large terrace are shared. Open May–Oct.

Boračko Lake Eco Village (106 beds; Boračko jezero; **☏** 033 200 249; **w** ekoselo.ba; 26–30KM pp B&B) Located on the shores of Boračko jezero 18km from Konjic, they have their own private access to the lake. The complex offers simple & comfortable accommodation, & has a large capacity for several types of clients. There are rustic, small wooden huts that sleep 2, a pair of log cabins that can sleep up to 8 people, & 5 larger log cabins that have 12 beds each. There is a restaurant & café-bar on the premises. Camping with tents or camper vans is also possible, with water & electric hook-ups available. It's an exceptionally pleasant place to relax in the shade & when it gets too hot, you can jump in the cool semi-glacier lake. The Eco Village organises activities such as rafting on the Neretva, & has large grounds that include football fields, volleyball courts on grass & sand, table tennis, rope climbing, darts, pool, kayaking, biking, & more. Open May–Oct.

🏠 **Boračko Lake Summer Garden/ Ljetna bašta Restaurant** (20 beds; Boračko jezero; **m** 061 648 840; **w** ljetnabasta.com; 22KM pp per night; breakfast 5KM) They offer an extensive dinner menu, but trout is their speciality. Average meal 14KM. Open May–Nov.

🏠 **Borašnica Camp at Boračko Lake** (100 beds; Boračko jezero; **m** 061 577 000; **w** borackojezero.ba; 20KM pp per night B&B, bungalow options 45–80KM) A large camp that organises rafting & Tito's bunker (page 55) tours. Open May–Oct.

FURTHER PRACTICALITIES This route has **three natural springs** and **one well**.

TRANSPORT There is local transport from the town of Konjic to Bijelimići throughout the year and frequently in the summer months.

▼ Boračko jezero is a semi-glacier lake popular with hikers and nature enthusiasts (AB)

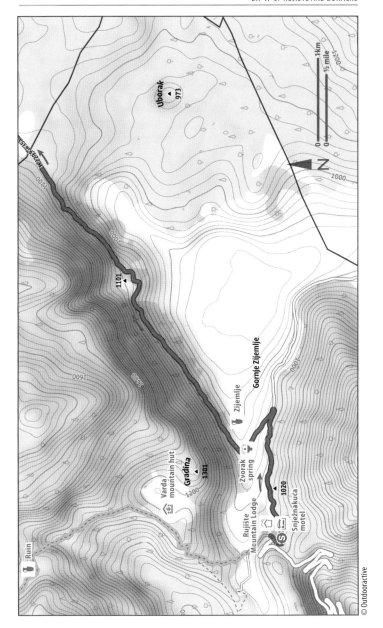

© Outdooractive

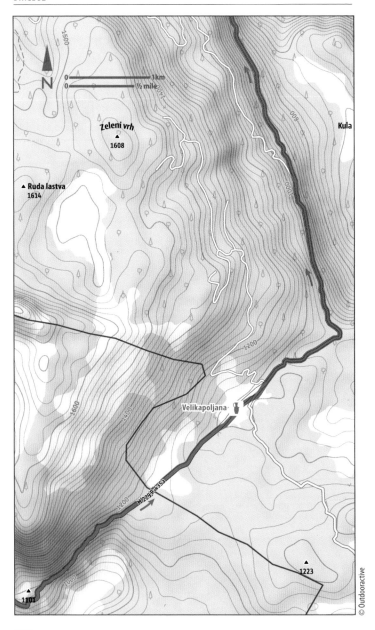

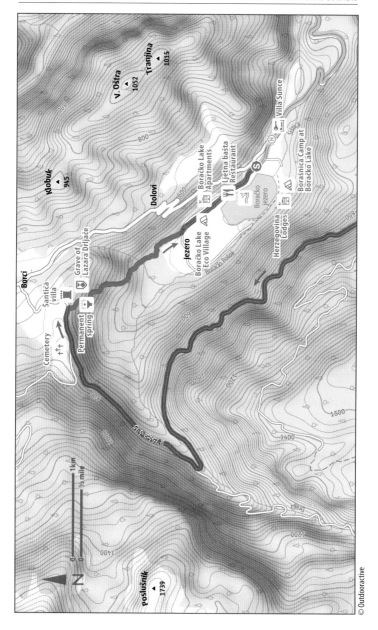

117

This hiking trail connects Boračko jezero with Lukomir village along the canyon of Rakitnica. It offers a great variety of terrain, passing through pastureland and forests, and offering exhilarating walking along the edge of Rakitnica Canyon, with excellent canyon views, and journeys through remote highland Bosnian villages.

Start Boračko jezero (417m)
Coordinates ⊗ Geogr 43.550924 N 18.036939 E/UTM 34T 260648 4826263
Finish Lukomir village (1,455m)
Difficulty difficult
Distance 32.5km
Duration 10hrs
Ascent 2,203m
Descent 1,161m

🚶 **THE ROUTE** This section of the Via Dinarica White Trail starts at Boračko jezero and follows the asphalt road generally southeast towards the village of Glavatičevo for the first few kilometres. On the left, towards the Neretva River, there will be a **suspension bridge**. The trail crosses the suspension bridge over the river and swings north, passing through the village of Kašići on its way up to the Šibenik and Kom rocky hills. In Kašići, turn right (north) and follow the track going uphill past the cemetery. At the top (T-junction), go left (north) and follow the trail down to Rakitnica Bridge. When approaching the confluence of the Neretva and Rakitnica rivers, keep right to reach the viewpoint above the confluence.

After crossing the river, the trail then enters a small area of woodland, then begins to climb, past the summit of Vis (796m), and along the ridge to follow the eastern slopes of Čepa (1,009m) ridge towards the north to the village of Dubočani, where it is said that the villagers were the last followers of the Bosnian Church to convert to Islam after the Ottomans had conquered Herzegovina. The trail joins the road above the village, and follows it for the next 2km or so, taking several directional changes and heading through pastures before entering an oak and beech forest. In the forest, the route turns sharply right (southeast) to climb over pathless terrain, and comes to the plateau above **Vranske stijene** (Crows' Rocks), at 1,299m along the canyon edge. It passes by an **old shepherd settlement (katun)** where an elderly couple still graze their sheep flock and cultivate

The village of **Lukomir** is perhaps the finest example of a highland village; it is the highest and most isolated permanent settlement in Bosnia and Herzegovina at 1,455m. The village, with its traditional architecture, has been deemed by the Historical Architecture Society of the United Kingdom as one of the longest continuously inhabited villages in all of Europe. The stone homes with cherry-wood roof shingles mark a practice that can no longer be found elsewhere on Bjelašnica.

The villagers are mainly shepherds who live off the sale of sheep products. Lukomir is known for its traditional attire as well, and the women still wear hand-knitted costume styles that have been worn for centuries. Electricity was introduced to the village and running water installation was completed in 2002. Access to the village is impossible between the first snows in December and late April, and sometimes even later, except by skis or on foot. Getting to Lukomir is complicated; you need an off-road vehicle to get close to it. There are no buses.

their garden in a very traditional way. The trail leaves the edge of the canyon and goes north, then northeast, through a forested area which ends in the open pasture lands of southern Bjelašnica Mountain. The **ruins of Blace village** are located close to the edge of the **Rakitnica Canyon**. From this point, the trail continues east and mainly follows the canyon rim, sometimes trending slightly into the beech forest to the north but always returning to the edge. After a short climb north through woodland, the trail again heads east, crossing the southern slopes of Mount Lovnica (1,856m), bringing you to the highest village in Bosnia: **Lukomir**, just below the peak of Vijenac (1,496m) and the finishing point of this stage. Here you'll have a chance to experience life as it was once upon a time all over the Bosnian and Herzegovinian highlands, but also how modern civilisation is easily taking over. The next stage of the trail starts at the southeastern corner of the village, close by the *stećci* necropolis and guesthouse.

This is a hard stage of the trail, in terms of both distance and climbing. Furthermore, no accommodation or places to eat can be found along the route, until reaching Lukomir; a tent, and plenty of food for this demanding day, may therefore need to be carried.

WHAT TO SEE Boračko jezero is a semi-glacial lake at an elevation of just over 400m, and is a leisure resort with an abundance of tourist infrastructure, most of which is functional during the warmest months of the year. A large section of the crystal-clear turquoise **Neretva River** is potable and the stretch of river between Boračko jezero and the

> 👁 **Rafting on the Neretva River** is an all-day adventure, and there
> are many rafting outfits to choose from. Some have better gear than
> others but they all provide you with breakfast and lunch (lunch is usually a
> barbecue somewhere deep in the Neretva Canyon) included in the price.
> The price is more or less standard and foreigners pay 100KM per person.
> Some operators (page 63) give group discounts.

village of Glavatičevo is a favourite white-water rafting spot (for further information on rafting on the Neretva River, see box, above).

The **Rakitnica Canyon** is the least-explored canyon in southern Europe. It stretches 26km and feeds the Neretva River in Herzegovina near Konjic. Rakitnica is a natural wonderland. Hundreds of thousands of years of tectonic shifts have created the steep limestone walls of Visočica and Bjelašnica mountains. The crystal-clear river below is fed by the melting snows and the hundreds of underground aquifer systems, making Rakitnica River water potable for the entire length of the canyon. Thirty-two endemic species of plants, flowers and trees can be found in this tiny region of the Dinaric Alps.

Blatačko jezero (Blatačko Lake) is located at an elevation of 1,150m; the water from this lake flows underground into the spectacular depths of Rakitnica Canyon below. 👁 **Lukomir** (see box, page 119) is situated at 1,455m and is one of the most isolated villages in the mountains of Bosnia and Herzegovina. It offers a rare peek into ancient European ways of living.

WHERE TO STAY AND EAT

🏠 **Natura AS Mountain house** (17 beds; Lukomir bb; **m** 061 918 324; **w** lukomir.com; 36KM pp B&B) Located in the remotest village in the country, on the slopes of Bjelašnica Mountain, at 1,495m. Rustic accommodation & excellent local food. Open May–Nov. Must book in advance.

🏠 **Lukomir Guesthouse** (12 beds; Lukomir; **m** 061 590 617; 25KM pp B&B) Offers traditional dishes made from local, organic products. Open Apr–Dec.

✕ **Ljetna bašta Restaurant** (Lukomir; **m** 061 590 617; 14KM average meal) This small mountain restaurant is located almost at the entrance to Lukomir village – the 2nd house on the right. Ljetna bašta Restaurant offers traditional dishes made with organic, local products.

FURTHER PRACTICALITIES Ask your host at Boračko to give you a ride to the suspension bridge on the Neretva. This saved hour will mean a lot later on in what is a long hiking day. There are **four natural springs** on this route, with three found within the first third of this stage. Water can be a problematic on this part so be sure to have enough with you.

A number of operators offer rafting on the Neretva River (KM)

THE LEGEND OF KONJIC

Long before the town of Konjic was established as a settlement, there was a small village tucked in the deep valley of Prenj Mountain near Boračko Lake. In this village lived a widow with her two children. One evening a lone traveller appeared in the village, tired and dirty from his journey. He asked several villagers for some food, drink and a place to sleep but, wary of foreigners, they turned him down. He eventually came to the door of the widow and she kindly let him in. As they were eating supper this mysterious vagabond told the widow of an imminent danger that would destroy the village. He warned her to leave at once, at first light, in order to save herself and the children. 'I have come as a messenger, and your fellow villagers have all turned me away.' He instructed her to gather her belongings and take her children on horses over the large mountain to the northwest. The man told her when her horse stopped and dug his hoof into the ground three times, this was the place she would be safe and should make her new home. When the woman awoke the next morning, the stranger was gone. She didn't know what to believe. She spoke to her neighbours and they laughed at her. She was frightened for her children and wanted to save her neighbours from the impending doom but they would not be convinced. The woman gathered her things and saddled her horses. The journey over the mountain took several days until she reached an open valley near a river. Her little horse bucked and jumped. Bowing to the ground the horse dug his hoof into the ground three times. At that moment, a large roar rolled down through the valley and the earth shook. It was here that she settled with her children as the man had instructed her. The little horse had led them to safety and a new life. The settlement of Konjic, began on this day. For more information on Konjic, see pages 55–6.

TRANSPORT There is local transport from the town of Konjic to Bjelimići. However, there are no public transport services once the suspension bridge at Kašići has been crossed.

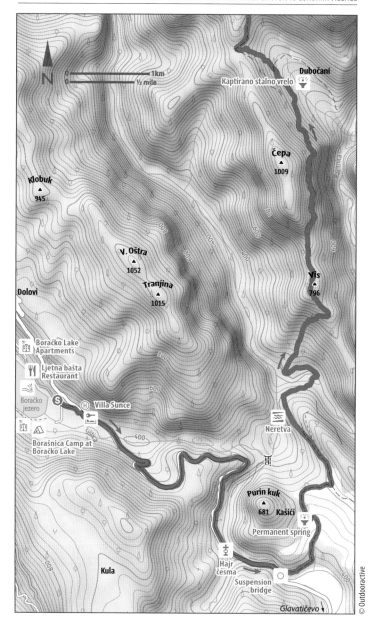

Dubočani
Kaptirano stalno vrelo

Čepa
▲
1009

Klobuk
▲
945

V. Oštra
▲
1052

Tranjina
▲
1015

Vis
▲
796

Dolovi

Boračko Lake
Apartments

Ljetna bašta
Restaurant

Boračko
jezero

Villa Sunce

Neretva

Borašnica Camp at
Boračko Lake

Purin kuk
▲
681   Kašići

Permanent spring

Hajr
česma

Kula

Suspension
bridge

Glavatičevo

© Outdooractive

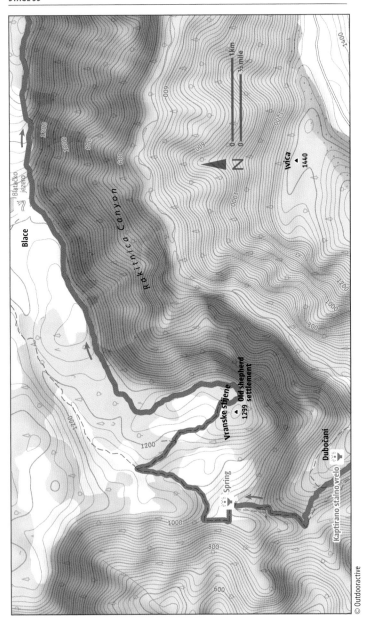

© Outdooractive

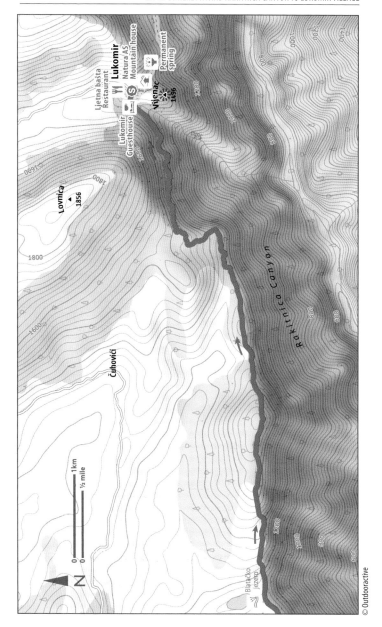

BH-W-09 LUKOMIR VILLAGE VIA VISOČICA MOUNTAIN TO LJUTA

This stage of the Via Dinarica is a popular one- or two-day section of the hiking trail that continues along the Rakitnica Canyon towards the highland village of Umoljani and crossing a number of high points including Visočica Mountain. You will pass through the attractive scenery of the Jelenjača and Ljuta valleys en route to Ljuta village. On this section of the trail is the most concentrated collection of small mountain communities with plenty of opportunities for village stays.

Start Lukomir village (1,455m)
Coordinates ⊕ Geogr 43.637160 N 18.183521 E/UTM 34T 272815 4835429
Finish Ljuta village (872m)
Difficulty difficult
Distance 30.4km
Duration 11hrs
Ascent 1,362m
Descent 1,959m

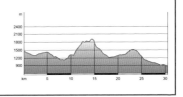

🥾 **THE ROUTE** From the village of Lukomir, near the old school house that now houses the Natura AS Mountain house, and medieval cemetery, the trail continues east along the canyon, beneath the Obalj massif to the north (1,896m). The route hugs the high end of the canyon for about 4.5km (1.5 hours' walking), before reaching the stream of **Studeni potok**. A large valley will open to the left (north). The trail crosses the creek where you turn right (east) towards the canyon again after a short distance, before the trail continues north; after 15–20 minutes of walking, you will reach the opposite side of the hill to a natural spring and seven **watermills** (the water is potable at this source). From this water source the trail descends down to the creek and veers right (east) towards the asphalt road. Umoljani Mosque is on the left. Follow the asphalt road north for just over 1km to the village of ⊙ **Umoljani** which is just over the hill to the left (northwest) and only a 10-minute walk from the mosque. It is well worth the visit for a cool drink or bite to eat. Many use Umoljani as a convenient hub to do day hikes and overnight in the village. The Lukomir–Umoljani section of this stage is around a 2.5-hour hike at a steady pace. For more information on Umoljani, see page 63.

To continue, the trail zigzags (the asphalt road can be followed for 1km or, alternatively, head down the valley near the **UNESCO World Heritage**

▲ Medieval stećci in the countryside near Umoljani village (AB)

Site medieval tombstones; for further information on these tombstones (*stećci*), see box, page 37.), before it descends southward to the bridge over the Rakitnica River. This part of the trail follows the asphalt road for another 0.5km or so, before a making a right (southwest) turn towards the village of 👁 **Bobovica**, with the peak of Prut (1,436m) to the west. There are clear and visible Via Dinarica markings at all these intersections. From Bobovica, continue for 2.5km straight towards **Drstva** (left (southerly) direction when facing the entrance to the village). From Drstva follow the pleasant high-level ridge trail for a further 2km south towards **Vito** peak at 1,960m, from where the trail descends left (southeast) to the scree slopes about 200m from the summit. The trail from here leads northeast all the way down into the Tušila Valley, where 🏠 **Vrela Mountain Lodge** (run by the Treskavica Mountain Association, and offering meals and accommodation) and other guesthouses are located.

At the end of the asphalt is a fork in the road. Take the road to the right (south) towards the village of Bjelimići. After climbing toward the saddle for about 20–30 minutes through the forest leave the road through the pasture on your right (west). During springtime there is a small lake here as a landmark. There are Via Dinarica signs at this intersection.

The trail again goes into the forest and continues south, following the bottom of the Jelenjača Valley up to the pass between the peaks of **Puzim** to the east and **Visočica** to the west. Along the trail on the south side is **Puzimsko Cemetery**. The trail is a forest track for a short while on its north side along the fence. Follow that road east which eventually opens to a network of forest tracks, but remain on the marked main track until the end. Continue over the bank and glade which follows and soon joins a new forest track. Be sure to stay on the main track as there are several clearly 'secondary' ones. After a short walk, the view to Treskavica Mountain will open up towards the east. From this spot take a right (east) turn downhill along the path. This trail will end on a proper forest road and descend, crossing a couple of rivers and passing by the hamlet of Vlahovići to the Ljuta River.

Cross the bridge at the river and turn up to the right (south and not hard right) on the upper road that leads to the hamlet of Budovići. The hamlet is a good place to take a break; there is also accommodation, at the Vladavić household located on the banks of the cool Palež Creek. The stage ends a short distance south at Ljuta village.

WHAT TO SEE This part of the trail is the heart of highland life around the capital city Sarajevo. About an hour's drive from Sarajevo, this area has over a dozen small mountain communities that very much live in the traditional way. In **Umoljani village** there is the **UNESCO World Heritage Site medieval tombstones** (*stećci*). The **Rakitnica Canyon** is one of the most wild, beautiful and unexplored in all of Europe. The views from **Vito summit** are no less than spectacular so be sure not to skip that part of the hike. **Studeni potok** is a meandering creek adjacent to the Rakitnica Canyon with impressive cascades that drop 300m into the Rakitnica River below, and are among the highest waterfalls in the Balkans. In the Tušila Valley there is a **bolted climbing rock** in the area which is popular with visitors and locals.

WHERE TO STAY AND EAT

🏠 **Studeno vrelo** (8 beds; Umoljani village; **m** 062 337 877; **f** StudenoVrelo; 50KM)
There is a restaurant just behind & up from the main water fountain in the middle of village. They also rent out a log cabin behind the restaurant.

The village of **Bobovica** sits high on the ridge above the Rakitnica Canyon, on the north slopes of Visočica Mountain. The village has stunning panoramic views of Bjelašnica, Visočica and Treskavica mountains, and there are well-maintained trails that travel deep into the steep canyon as well as to the high, sharp peaks of Visočica. It is situated above the valley of the Tušilačka River, which is a tributary of the Rakitnica River. The area around the village is famous for its beautiful meadows, covered with wildflowers in the spring. Much of the village has been restored in traditional style.

During Ottoman times, **Umoljani**, a small village in the Bjelašnica highlands had to face its own demons. There were rumours of a dragon-like creature roaming the foothills of Obalj Mountain. Some shepherds swore they saw it, others claimed to have lost sheep to the creature. The villagers were panic-stricken. The local Muslim priest (*hodža*) decided to go and find this dragon. He expected to find nothing but asked the villagers to pray for him while he was gone. For days, there was no sign of the *hodža* and the scared villagers diligently prayed. Then, as the tale goes, the *hodža* met the beast just above the shepherds' summer huts. He, too, used prayer as his main weapon, and in an instant the dragon was frozen in stone on top of the mountain. The *hodža* returned with news that he had defeated the dragon. He gave credit to the faith and prayers of the villagers for his impossible victory and named the village Umoljani, meaning 'Of the prayers'. On a peak just above the village of Umoljani is a rock formation that very much resembles a dragon.

🏠 **Pansion Umoljani** (30 beds; Umoljani village; m 061 228 142; e umoljani@gmail.com; www.umoljani.com.ba; 40KM). A basic but comfortable and clean B&B with en suite rooms available. The restaurant serves very good local dishes and the service is friendly.

🏠 **Oko Treskavice household** (10 beds; Budovići village; m 061 923 486; 16KM pp B&B) This household offers great gastro specialities like fresh brown trout & different savoury pies baked in a 'sač' oven, as well as homemade cheeses, honey & handpicked organic herbal teas. Open on weekends throughout the year. Recommended to call for weekday visits.

🏠 **Vrela Lodge** (30 beds; Tušila village; ☏ 033 239 031; from 14KM pp per night) The lodge is located at 1,210m, has a large kitchen for up to 50 guests, & basic amenities such as running water, electricity, toilets & phone. Open year-round.

✕ **Koliba** (m 061 511 323; ◼ kolibaumoljani; 10–20KM) This is the best restaurant in Umoljani just past the main graveyard on the road to the summer settlement of Gradina & Studeno Polje. This family owned & operated eatery has great traditional dishes & the best views in the village. Try the barley stew.

FURTHER PRACTICALITIES There are no shops in this area but there are a handful of small B&Bs and local eateries. There are a number of **water sources** along the trail which should be taken advantage of on this long stage.

TRANSPORT There is public transport from the Sarajevo suburb of Ilidža at the main tram/bus station, via Maršal, Šabići, Umoljani (in the vicinity) and Bobovica (in the vicinity), to the village of Sinanovići twice per day in summer and once per day in the winter. Schedules vary.

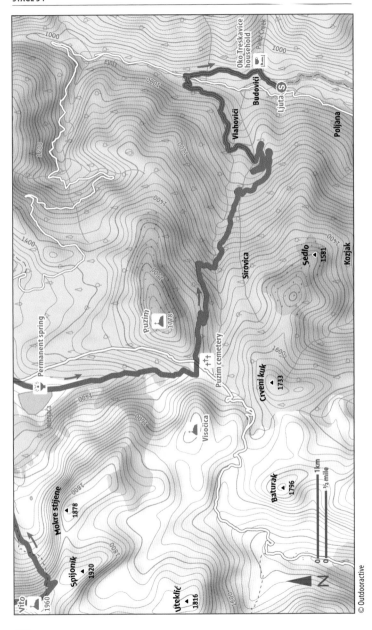

© Outdooractive

▲ Studeno polje (Frosty Field), just above the village of Umoljani (OL)

▼ A 500-year-old highland mosque, the oldest mountain mosque in BiH, in the ancient village of Umoljani (AB)

From the Ljuta Valley, this stage of the Via Dinarica follows a forest road and mountain trail, with gravel underfoot for most of the way, to the town of Kalinovik by hiking or mountain biking. The hiking tour goes over the southern slopes of Treskavica and Lukavac summit to Vlaholje village. Alternatively, you can choose to take this stage by bike directly to Kalinovik along the gravel track to gain some time to explore this tiny highland town. Hiking to Lukavac and Treskač is also highly recommended.

Start Ljuta village (872m)
Coordinates ⊕ Geogr 43.578774 N 18.305240 E/UTM 34T 282423 4828618
Finish Jelašca village (1,121m)
Difficulty moderate
Distance 30.9 km
Duration 12hrs
Ascent 1,255m
Descent 992m

🚶 THE ROUTE Bike or hike the gravel road for 10km in a largely southeasterly direction to the crossing to Jakomišlje. There, turn left (east) on to a trail going into the beech forest. There are signs indicating this turn-off. The trail then climbs up to just below the summit of **Lukavac** (1,768m). The summit of Lukavac is just 10 minutes' detour from the main trail, so, being the highest point that can be reached on this stage, it is recommended you visit it and then return to the same point. Having returned to the main trail, continue eastward, traversing the northern slopes of Orlov kuk (1,712m). Follow the trail to a seasonal stream crossing, a short distance after which you should turn left (northeast) towards Nenkovci village. At the crossing after that, do not continue to Nenkovci, but turn right (south) to Vlaholje village. The trail descends to Vlaholje and the first houses you pass are Simovica houses (Simovića kuće), where you can stay overnight. Near the next house turn left (south) on to the trail, instead of continuing on the road. This trail brings you back to the road; turn right there and cross the stream, then turn left after the cemetery. Follow that road the rest of the way to Kalinovik and watch for the sign pointing to Vezac Fortress, if you want to visit the site. In the centre of Kalinovik, the trail goes left (southeast), following the main road towards Sarajevo and Foča. After the fuel station, you will spot abandoned buildings and structures on the right side of the road.

Here, you should turn right (east) through the gate and continue on the road through this ex-military facility to the next gate. Join a dirt road that will bring you into open, grassy fields; somewhere near the centre of the field there is a medieval necropolis (*stećci*) known as **Mirkova kosa**, and it is just 100m from the road, so it is worth visiting. This dirt road brings you to Jelašca village, where this stage of the trail ends. There is one B&B here to overnight at the 🏠 **Lalović household**. Camping in the fields is also acceptable but it's always best to ask the landowner (see below). The next stage will continue by following the regional road towards Ćemerno.

WHAT TO SEE **Ljuta village** is an idyllic, picture-book village nestled in the mountains, where local residents offer freshly caught trout from the stream and organic vegetables straight from the garden. **Jelašca village** is a small village near Kalinovik, close to Mount Lelija (2,032m). The now-ruined **mosque in Jelašca village** was built on the foundation of an Orthodox church. The mosque was destroyed in World War II. In the courtyard blossoms beautiful linden, planted by King Milutin 700 ago, at the same time as when the church was built.

🏠 WHERE TO STAY AND EAT
🏠 **Hotel Moskva** (60 beds; Sumadijska bb, Kalinovik; ☎ 057 623 202; w hotelmoskvakalinovik.com; 40KM pp B&B) The only hotel in Kalinovik, the Moskva has a sauna & an indoor pool. Open year-round. Advisable to book in advance.

🏠 **B&B at Lalović family** (18 beds; Jelašca bb, Kalinovik; m 065 241 951; 20KM pp B&B) A unique, custom-made wooden lodging built by the owner. Organic, homemade meals. Open year-round. A large campsite available next to the house; 5–10KM per tent.

🏠 **B&B Simovića kuće** (8 beds; Vlaholje bb, Kalinovik; m 065 442 213; 20KM pp B&B) This family-owned household is comfortable & includes all necessities for an overnight stay. They offer excellent guiding services for the area & transport by 4x4 vehicle. Open all year. Advisable to book in advance.

FURTHER PRACTICALITIES For further assistance regarding this stage of the Via Dinarica trail, contact **Lelija Mountain Club** in Kalinovik (m 065 762 703; e novak. g959@teol.ne).

There is no public transport locally.

▶ Organic honey production has a long tradition in the Ljuta River Valley (OL)

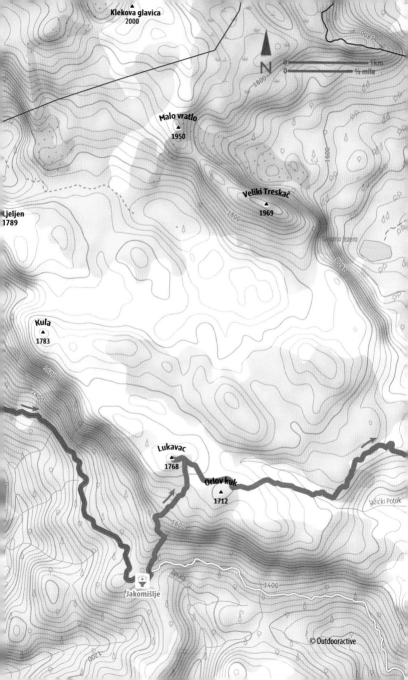

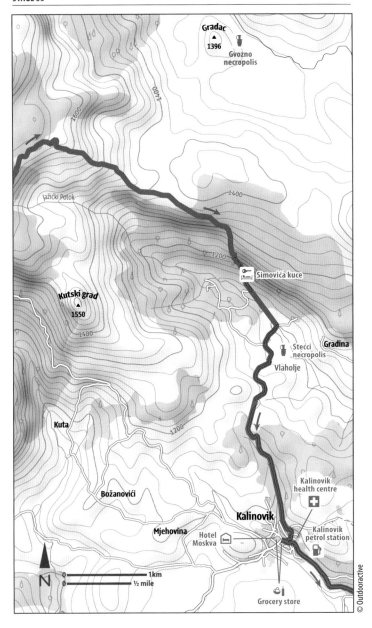

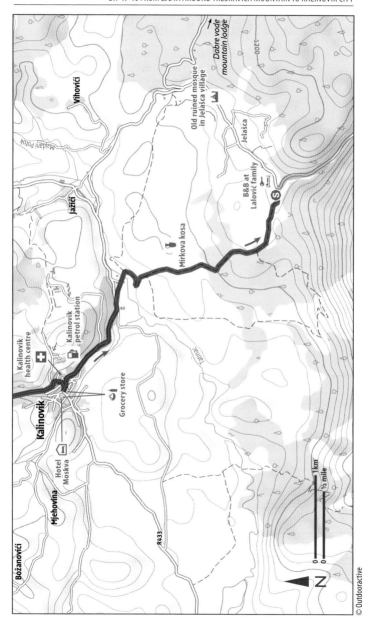

© Outdooractive

🚏 BH-W-11 VIA LELIJA AND ZELENGORA MOUNTAIN TO SUTJESKA NATIONAL PARK

This is a great mountain hike through pristine nature over Lelija and Zelengora that includes three summits and five lakes. It is one of the most remote areas of the Via Dinarica White Trail in Bosnia and Herzegovina. The trail system here is well marked and visible but it is vital to be a smart hiker in this kind of terrain.

Start Jelašca village (1,121m)
Coordinates ⊕ Geogr 43.480798 N 18.477877 E/UTM 34T 296032 4817299
Finish Donje Bare Mountain Hut (1,488m)
Difficulty difficult
Distance 37.4km
Duration 14hrs
Ascent 2,145m
Descent 1,766m

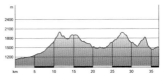

🚶 **THE ROUTE** The trail follows the forest road (the once-regional dirt road) towards Čemerno village (turning right (south) at the T-junction at the south end of Jelašca village) and Orlovačko jezero (Orlovačko Lake), and in Ošlji do turns towards Lelija Mountain. At the junction near the Lalović family B&B (page 135), follow the road southeast for around 6km to **Ošlji do**, and turn right (south) at the junction with the big information board 'Dr Jovo Elčić Mountain Trail'. Once in the open area, continue along the road to the left all the way to the end. (It is more pleasant to walk along the meadow parallel with the road, and join the road at the end.) At the end of the road, continue southwest on the trail which is clearly marked. There is an opportunity to refill water bottles at the **Jablan vrelo** spring, even though there is also another water source a short distance beyond, beneath Lelija summit.

There is a junction on the shoulder of Lelija, where the trail continues straight south (the summit is to the right to the highest point of Lelija Mountain, **Velika Lelija** (2,032m), and left down is to Poda locality). The trail continues south through very remote and wild terrain. The next crossing is close by **Jović vrelo** (Jović spring). At a long stretch of mountain meadow, the trail veers south uphill over even more difficult terrain, before descending to **Štirine** – a remnant of an old shepherd settlement and **Štirinsko jezero** (Štirinsko Lake).

Just before the lake, go east. The next lake along the trail, after a further 5km, is **Jugovo jezero** (Jugovo Lake, also known as Borilovacko

▲ Bregoč Peak on Zelengora Mountain in Sutjeska National Park (KM)

Lake), which is elongated in a north–south direction. Soon after passing the lake, heading east, you will come to the road. Turn left on the road, passing a **mountain hut**, and continue along it to **Orlovačko jezero** (Orlovačko Lake). There will be one more junction before the lake: turn right (east) there. Orlovačko is a nice place for a break. From the lake, continue southeast, then south, on the trail. From here, the trail climbs to the highest summit of 👁 Zelengora – **Bregoč**. There will be a few paths going left or right, but remain on the one going straight up. When you reach the T-junction go left, and the next right will be towards the summit of Bregoč. After Bregoč the trail continues south over open terrain, to the end of the plateau and descends through a

👁 With its highest point at the summit of Bregoč (2,014m), **Zelengora Mountain** on the edge of Sutjeska National Park is great for hiking and walking and there are several newly renovated mountain huts on its slopes. Bear and wolf sightings are common.

steep and exposed gully. From there, the trail leads eastward into the forest where it is quite clear to follow, then again through high Alpine meadows (upon exiting the forest you may not see markings in the open area), then, with clear trail markings again, climbs southeast to Uglješa peak (Uglješin vrh) at 1,859m.

Leaving Uglješin Vrh, the trail descends on the opposite side to **Gornje Bare Lake**. While you are above the lake you will notice the track leading to the road, so follow it until the end. When you meet the road, follow it to the crossing, then turn right towards **Donje Bare Lake**. There are signs at these intersections. At Donje Bare there is a park-managed **mountain hut**. Be sure to contact the Sutjeska National Park to reserve accommodation at the hut in advance. There are open fields for camping as well. This is where your long Zelengora journey ends.

The ⌂ **mountain hut** at Orlovačko jezero is the only accommodation situated along what is a long and demanding mountain stage. It may therefore be deemed necessary to carry a tent, and sufficient food.

WHAT TO SEE Zelengora mountain range is a lovely part of **Sutjeska National Park**, and is home to nine crystal-clear lakes. These include two lakes: **Borilovačko** at 1,450m and **Orlovačko** at 1,438m, which are only 1km apart, as well as the lake at the tranquil **Donje Bare** at 1,475m, surrounded by beech forests. Further on from Donje Bare, you stand the chance of spotting a bear; although wolves are in the area, sightings are rare. **Bregoč** is the highest peak on Zelengora, at 2,014m.

⌂ WHERE TO STAY AND EAT
⌂ **Mountain hut at Donje Bare Lake** (4 beds; Donje Bare, Tjentište; ☏ 058 233 130; 105KM daily house rental only + 5KM one-time fee) Bring food. A small hut located at 1,488m on Donje Bare Lake. Open May–Oct (depending on snow conditions); call in advance.

⌂ **Mountain hut at Orlovačko Lake** (4 beds; Orlovačko, Tjentište; ☏ 058 233 130; 105KM daily house rental only + 5KM one-time fee) Located at 1,490m, no electricity. A large campsite nearby, 130 people capacity, 10KM/day. Open May–Oct (depending on snow conditions); call in advance.

FURTHER PRACTICALITIES For further information on **Sutjeska National Park** (w npsutjeska.info), see the following stage and also page 64.

TRANSPORT There is no public transport in this region.

The Gornje Bare Lake and views of Maglić on Zelengora Mountain (KM)

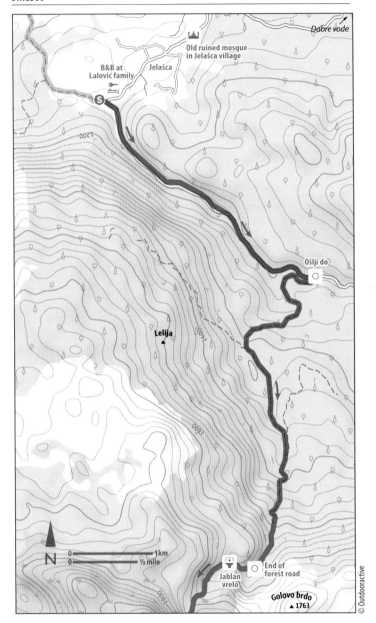

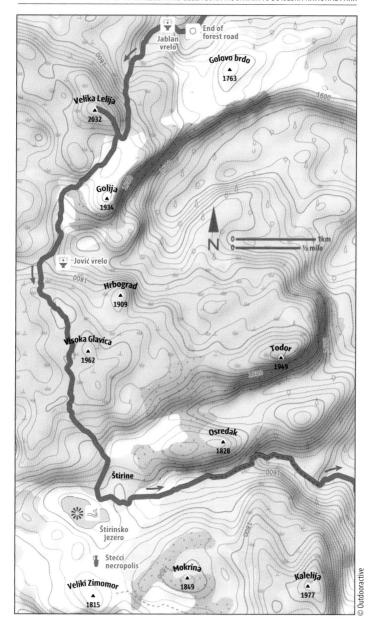

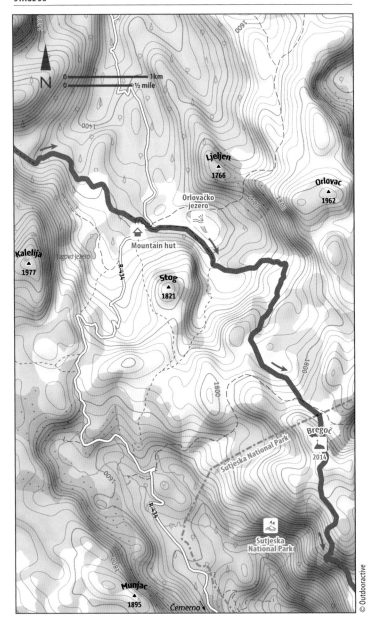

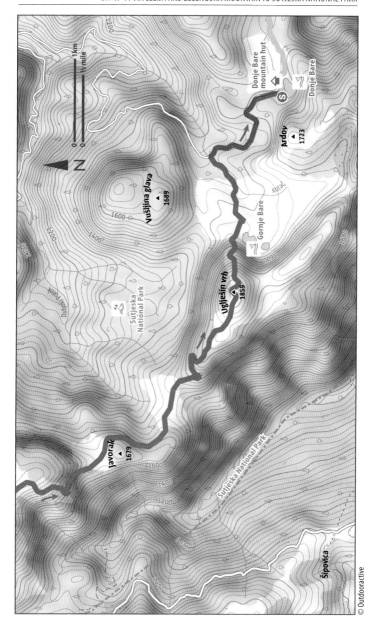

This trail connects Zelengora and Maglić within Sutjeska National Park.
This is some of the most beautiful terrain on the White Trail in Bosnia
and Herzegovina. The hike from Donje Bare to Prijevor will take at least
5 hours and from there it is optional on whether or not to overnight in
the katuni huts or to carry on to Trnovačko jezero (Trnovačko Lake) in
Montenegro just an hour and a half away before ascending to Maglić
Mountain – Bosnia and Herzegovina's highest peak.

It is recommended to reserve a night at the hut in Prijevor, and travel to
Trnovačko jezero and do the Maglić ascent the next day. The ascent from
Prijevor is challenging, but a great accomplishment.

Start Donje Bare mountain hut (1,488m)
Coordinates ⊕ Geogr 43.318777 N 18.629894 E/UTM 34T 307814
4798943
Finish Trnovačko jezero (1,517m)
Difficulty moderate
Distance 20.5km
Duration 8hrs
Ascent 1,285m
Descent 1,225m

🏃 **THE ROUTE** From the lake at **Donje Bare**, continue east along an open meadow for around 10 minutes, and you will reach a junction from where you can turn right (south) to visit **Borić viewpoint**. This small but worthwhile detour is about an hour's round trip.

To reach the main trail again, return to the junction and follow the sign pointing northeast towards Kovačev Panj. This is the main trail down into the valley. The trail descends through a grassy meadow before leading into a thick beech tree forest. Although this path is not frequently used, the markings are good and visible, and the path is very obvious and easy to follow. Once you've entered the forest it is a 2-hour hike (mostly descending) until you reach the main road going through the Tjentište Valley. The administration centre, campgrounds, info centre, hotel and restaurant of the **Sutjeska National Park** are located 4km from the trail after you've hit the main road. To continue along the Via Dinarica White Trail, however, turn right (southeast) on the main road in the direction of Dubrovnik, heading south for around 2.5km to rejoin the hiking trail from Suha Valley.

The trail then leaves the road on the left (east) from the parking area at Suha and follows the forest road for a while. Very soon the road will make a sharp turn left (north); there, you should continue straight following the white and red trail markers, taking the short cut through the forest. In the forest, you will pass a **park watchtower** before getting on the forest road again. Some 20m after that, you will encounter a sign showing you a path towards a ridge up above. This point is only about a 20 minute walk from the Suha gate near the main road. The ridge leads you east towards Prijevor, a pass beneath Mount Maglić, the highest summit of Bosnia and Herzegovina (2,386m). The trail then goes steeply uphill (east) all the way to the ridge. Approximately 1 hour later, you should reach a new junction. The left path to the north leads down into ◉ **Perućica primeval forest** and should be avoided because special permits are required to enter this forest reserve. Take the right path, which follows the ridge in a southeasterly direction. Orientation shouldn't be difficult as the path is very visible and follows along the ridge until reaching the **Prijevor Pass** which is a long alpine meadow below the peak of Maglić Mountain. At one point, the path comes to a flat part of the ridge and may be harder to see, but looking to the right should direct you towards the end of the ridge where the path is more overgrown by young trees and shrubs. After passing near the second watchtower in an open alpine meadow, you will reach the road and parking area at Prijevor with the peak of **Maglić** (2,386m) dominating the landscape in the background.

▼ A birds-eye view of Trnovačko Lake in Montenegro near Bosnia's highest peak, Maglić (AB)

SUTJESKA NATIONAL PARK

Sutjeska is one of Bosnia and Herzegovina's oldest parks. It is famous for the Partisan victory over the Germans in World War II and there are large stone monuments commemorating the event. The park itself is 16,500ha of magnificent wilderness.

The Sutjeska River has carved a stunning valley through the middle of the park. Bosnia and Herzegovina's highest peak at 2,386m, Maglić is located in the park, directly on the border with Montenegro, and presents a challenging climb for experienced hikers. Despite their diminished numbers, it is not uncommon to see a bear, or occasionally a wolf.

The national park has managed to maintain its pristine nature and in terms of marked paths, good maps or visitor information, there has been much improvement over the years.

Sutjeska National Park is the main trailhead for the Via Dinarica trail, and guides from the park can be hired for 50KM per day.

You can refill your water bottle beneath the parking area at the westernmost point, as there is a **source of fresh water** that exists all year long.

From here, the trail goes south, following the dirt road where some **shepherd's huts** can be seen. At a few spots, the road is taken away by rockslides and some 30 minutes after leaving Prijevor, the road divides into two paths. Both paths will get you down to the **Suva jezerina pond**, but the one on the right, which pitches downhill, will take you to the crossing that has a sign pointing left towards **Trnovačko jezero** (Trnovačko Lake), and the end of the BiH section of the Via Dinarica White Trail. You'll reach the lake in less than 30 minutes from here. The border with Montenegro is on the other side of the Suva Jezerina. Be sure to have your passport with you when crossing into Montenegro. There is no official border crossing but there is a ranger from the Montenegrin side who occasionally checks the documents of hikers.

WHAT TO SEE Sutjeska National Park is the oldest and largest national park in Bosnia and Herzegovina. There are a handful of must-sees while in the park. 👁 **Perućica Nature Reserve** is home to one of the last remaining primeval forests in Europe, and where any element of human intervention has been forbidden since the National Park was established. There are a number of impressive mountains: **Volujak**, **Vučevo**, **Zelengora** and **Maglić**, the last of which is the highest peak in Bosnia and Herzegovina, at 2,386m. There are two highly recommended viewpoints: Borić viewpoint, from where you can see the Sutjeska River Canyon, the mountains of Vučevo, Maglić and Volujak, Perućica rainforest, the mountain passes of Dragoš sedlo and Prijevor, the Tjentište Valley, and remnants of the ancient cities of Vratar and Vrata; and Prijevor viewpoint at 1,668m, from where Maglić towers overhead and a whole chain of Dinaric peaks spreads in front of you. There also two lakes: **Donje Bare**, a lake on Zelengora Mountain; and **Trnovačko jezero** (Trnovačko Lake) at 1,517m, which lays beneath the heights of Maglić and is best known for its heart-like shape and deep green-blue colour.

WHERE TO STAY AND EAT

Hotel Mladost (40+ rooms; Sutjeska National Pk, Tjentište bb; ☎ 058 233 118; e info@npsutjeska.net; w npsutjeska.net; 60KM pp per night). Situated 3.25km from the trailhead from Kovačev Panj, this 3-star hotel is the only accommodation in the park with facilities. It offers decent accommodation and services. Some rooms have been renovated, so when booking, be sure to ask for one of those.

Mountain huts on Prijevor (16 beds; Tjentište; ☎ 058 233 130; 27KM pp per night + 5KM one-time fee) These 3 small, traditional summer huts (*katuni*), located at the foot of Maglić Mountain at 1,700m, have been recently restored to accommodate hikers. Although they are just huts with bunkbeds, toilet & basic shower, the location & views are stupendous & are worth sacrificing small material luxuries to see. It is possible to pre-order meals at good prices, but you are advised to bring your own food. The closest shop is quite a way down the mountain, so be sure to stock up. No electricity. The road from the Tjentište Valley to Katuni is gravel most of the way & not always in the best of shape. ☉ May–Oct (depending on snow conditions); call in advance.

FURTHER PRACTICALITIES

Sutjeska National Park 73311 Tjentište; ☎ 058 233 102; e npsutjeska@yahoo.com; w npsutjeska.info.

TRANSPORT The National Park Authority can arrange pickup and drop-off at both Donje Bare and Prijevor. Make reservations ahead of time if possible.

Hidden below Bosnia and Herzegovina's highest peak, Maglić Mountain, lies the magical valley home of **Perućica Nature Reserve** in Sutjeska National Park. Perhaps the most precious of all the forests, Perućica is one of the two remaining primeval forests in the whole of Europe. Massive beech trees are complemented by the high black pines on the rock faces that surround the valley. A hike through the heart of these woodlands is an unforgettable and awe-inspiring experience.

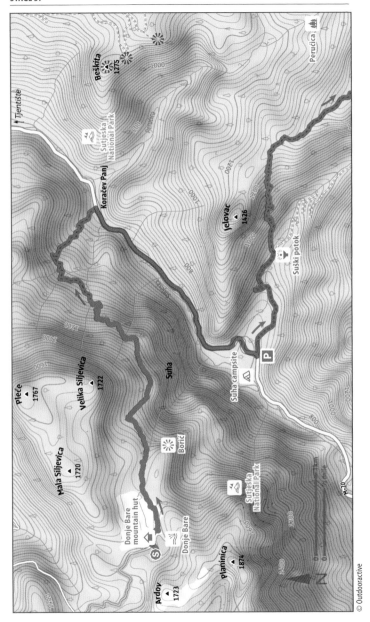

© Outdooractive

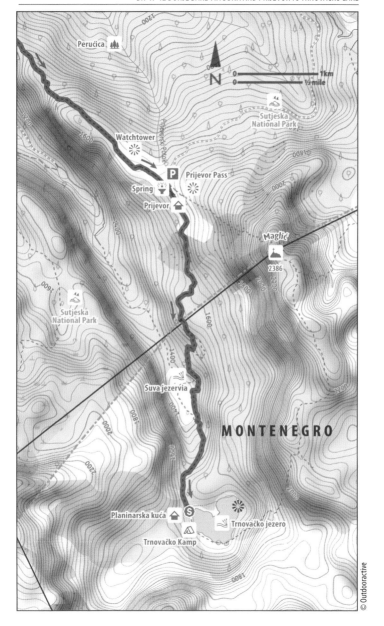

Perućica

Sutjeska
National Park

Watchtower

Prijevor Pass

Spring

Prijevor

Maglić
2386

Sutjeska
National Park

Suva jezervia

MONTENEGRO

Planinarska kuća

Trnovačko jezero

Trnovačko Kamp

© Outdooractive

153

Appendix 1

LANGUAGE

PRONUNCIATION

Latin	Cyrillic	Pronunciation
A, a	А, а	as in father
B, b	Б, б	as in bats
C, c	Ц, ц	as in Betsy
Č, č	Ч, ч	as in culture
Ć, ć	Ћ, ћ	as in cheese
D, d	Д, д	as in doctor
Dž, dž	Џ, џ	as in judge
Đ, đ	Ђ, ђ	as in duke
E, e	Е, е	as in pet
F, f	Ф, ф	as in free
G, g	Г, г	as in goat
H, h	Х, х	as in hat
I, i	И, и	as in feet
J, j	Ј, ј	as in yet
K, k	К, к	as in kept
L, l	Л, л	as in leg
Lj, lj	Љ, љ	as in million
M, m	М, м	as in mother
N, n	Н, н	as in no
Nj, nj	Њ, њ	as in onion
O, o	О, о	as in hot
P, p	П, п	as in pie
R, r	Р, р	as in rabbit (but rolled)
S, s	С, с	as in sand
Š, š	Ш, ш	as in shovel
T, t	Т, т	as in too
U, u	У, у	as in look
V, v	В, в	as in very
Z, z	З, з	as in zoo
Ž, ž	Ж, ж	as in treasure

154

GREETINGS

Good morning	*Dobro jutro*	Hello/Goodbye	*Ćao*
Good afternoon	*Dobar dan*	What is your name?	*Kako se zovete?*
Good evening	*Dobra večer*	How are you?	*Kako si?*
Good night	*Laku noć*	I am well	*Dobro sam*

BASIC PHRASES

please	*molim vas*	too much	*previše*
thank you	*hvala*	what?	*šta?*
you're welcome	*nema na čemu* (reply to thank you)	what's this (called)?	*kako se kaže?*
		who?	*ko?*
there is no	*nema*	when?	*kada?*
excuse me	*oprostite/izvinite*	where?	*gdje?*
give me	*dajte mi*	from where?	*odakle?*
I like to	*želim*	do you know?	*znate li?*
I would like	*želio bih*	I don't know	*ne znam*
how?	*kako?*	I don't understand	*ne razumijem*
how much/many?	*koliko?*	good	*dobrar/dobra/dobro* (m/f/n)
how much (cost)?	*koliko košta?*		

NUMBERS

one	*jedan*	nine	*devet*
two	*dva*	ten	*deset*
three	*tri*	eleven	*jedanaest*
four	*četiri*	twelve	*dvanaest*
five	*pet*	twenty	*dvadeset*
six	*šest*	thirty-one	*trideset i jedan*
seven	*sedam*	one hundred	*stotina*
eight	*osam*	one thousand	*hiljada*

NATURE AND SURROUNDINGS

river	*rijeka*	pass	*sedlo*
stream	*potok*	canyon	*kanjon*
water source	*izvor vode*	trail	*staza*
lake	*jezero*	gravel road	*makadam*
mountain	*planina*	forest	*šuma*

DIRECTIONS

descent	*padina*	west	*zapad*
ascent	*uspon*	north	*sjever*
east	*istok*	south	*jug*

SAFETY AND ASSISTANCE

first aid	*prva pomoć*	dry	*suho*
injured	*povreda, povrijeđen*	mountain hut	*planinski dom*
mountain rescue	*Gorska služba za spašavanje*	private accommodation	*privatni smještaj*
		B&B	*pansion*
wet	*mokro*	shelter	*sklonište*

EQUIPMENT

shoelaces	*pertle/vezice*	tent	*šator*
sunscreen	*krema za sunce*	hiking boots	*gojzderice*
lighter	*upaljač*	walking sticks	*štapovi za planiranje*
map	*karta/mapa*		
mobile signal	*signal za mobitel*	hat	*kapa/šešir*
campground	*kamp*	backpack	*ruksak*
		water bottle	*boca za voda*

HELPFUL PHRASES

I am lost	*Ja sam se izgubio*	I need water	*Treba mi voda*
I need directions	*Trebaju mi upute*	I need a break	*Treba mi pauza*
I need help	*Trebam pomoć*	I need some rest	*Trebam se odmoriti*

FOOD AND DRINK

baked	*pečeno*	fish	*riba*
bean	*grah*	fried	*prženo*
beef	*govedina/junetina*	fruit	*voće*
beer	*pivo*	grilled	*sa roštilja*
boiled	*kuhano*	homemade	*domaće*
bon appetit	*prijatno*	juice	*dus/sok*
brandy	*loza*	lamb	*jagnjetina/ janjetina*
bread	*hljeb/kruh*		
breakfast	*doručak*	lemon	*limun*
cabbage	*kupus/zelja*	lunch	*ručak*
cake	*kolač/torta*	meat	*meso*
cheese	*sir*	milk	*mlijeko*
chicken	*piletina*	onion	*luk*
chips, French fries	*pomfrit*	orange	*naranča/narandža*
coffee	*kafa/kahva*	pasta	*tjestinina*
cucumber	*krastavac*	peaches	*breskve*
dinner	*večera*	pears	*kruške*
drink (noun)	*piće*	plums	*šljive*
drink (verb)	*piti*	pork	*svinjetina*
eggs	*jaja*	potato	*krompir*

restaurant	*restoran*	to eat	*jesti*
rice	*riža/pirinač*	tomato	*paradajz*
salt	*so*	veal	*teletina*
soup	*supa/juha*	vegetables	*povrće*
spirit	*rakija*	water	*voda*
sugar	*šećer*	wine	*vino*
tea	*čaj*		

SHOPPING

bank	*banka*	postcard	*razglednica*
bookshop	*knjižara*	post office	*pošta*
chemist	*apoteka*	shop	*prodavaonica/*
market	*tržnica*		*trgovina*
money	*pare/novac*	toilet paper	*toalet papir*

GETTING AROUND

ahead/behind	*naprijed/iza*	petrol	*benzin*
departure/arrival	*polazak/dolazak/*	petrol station	*benzinska pumpa*
bus	*autobus*	plane/airport	*avion/aerodrom*
bus station	*autobusna stanica*	road/bridge	*cesta/most*
car/taxi	*auto/taxi*	straight on	*pravo*
east/west	*istok/zapad*	train	*voz*
entrance/exit	*ulaz/izlaz*	train station	*željeznička stanica*
here/there	*ovdje/tamo*	under/over	*ispod/iznad*
hill/mountain	*brdo/planina*	up/down	*gore/dole*
left/right	*lijevo/desno*	village/town	*selo/grad*
near/far	*blizu/daleko*	waterfall	*vodopad/slap*
north/south	*sjever/jug*		
open/closed	*otvoreno/zatvoreno*		

TIME

hour/minute	*sat/minuta*	Tuesday	*utorak*
week/day	*sedmica/dan*	Wednesday	*srijeda*
year/month	*godina/mjesec*	Thursday	*četvrtak*
now	*sada*	Friday	*petak*
soon	*uskoro*	Saturday	*subota*
today/tomorrow	*danas/sutra*	Sunday	*nedelja*
yesterday	*jučer*	spring	*proljeće*
morning	*jutro*	summer	*ljeto*
afternoon	*poslijepodne*	autumn	*jesen*
evening/night	*večer/noć*	winter	*zima*
Monday	*ponedeljak*		

OTHER USEFUL WORDS

a little	*malo*	key	*ključ*
a lot	*puno*	lake	*jezero*
after	*poslije*	large	*veliko*
bathroom	*kupatilo*	lorry	*kamion*
bed	*krevet*	mosque	*džamija*
before	*prije*	never	*nikad*
buildings	*zgrade*	night	*noć*
child	*dijete*	nightclub	*diskoteka*
church	*crkva*	nothing	*ništa*
cold	*hladno*	police	*policija*
currency	*valuta*	rain	*kiša*
dry	*suho*	river	*rijeka*
embassy	*ambasada*	room	*soba*
enough	*dosta*	sea	*more*
film	*film*	small	*malo*
hot/warm	*vruće/toplo*	street	*ulica*
hotel	*hotel*	to swim	*plivati*
house	*kuća*	tourist office	*turistički ured*
hut	*koliba*	you	*Vi/ti*

HEALTH WORDS AND PHRASES

dentist	*zubar*
doctor	*doktor*
fever	*groznica*
hospital	*bolnica*
ill	*bolestan*
to hurt	*boljeti*
I need a doctor	*Trebam doktora*
Please call an ambulance	*Molim Vas, pozovite hitnu pomoć*
I'm feeling dizzy	*Vrti mi se*
I ate something bad	*Pojeo (m)/Pojela (f) sam nešto loše*
I don't feel well	*Ne osjećam se dobro*
I have a headache	*Boli me glava*
My stomach hurts	*Boli me želudac*
I am allergic to penicillin	*Alergičan (m)/Alergična (f) sam na pencilin*
Where is the pharmacy	*Gdje je apoteka*
I forgot my prescription	*Zaboravio (m)/Zaboravila (f) sam svoj recept*

Appendix 2

FURTHER INFORMATION

WEBSITES

W viadinarica.com The official website of the Via Dinarica

W outdooractive.com Europe's largest outdoor platform, with maps, apps and info on hiking in the entire region

W viadinarica.hr The official website of the Via Dinarica trails in Croatia

W dinarskogorje.com A local website dedicated to the Dinaric Alps mountain chain

W summitpost.org An international hiking site with maps, highlights, photos and trip descriptions of trails worldwide

W via-dinarica.org The official site of the Via Dinarica Alliance, which is a consortium of private tour operators offering guided tours along the Via Dinarica

W npsutjeska.info The official site of the Sutjeska National Park

MAPS AND APPS

W viadinarica.com

W openfietsmap.nl/downloads/europe

W libricon.hr/Prenj---karta-1--40-0000_b280.aspx

W buy.garmin.com/en-GB/GB/p/566315

W outdooractive.com/en/mobile.html

Windows on
EUROPE

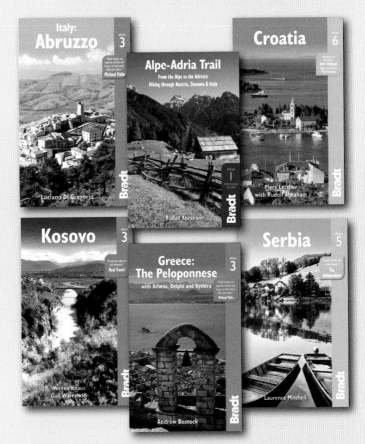

Bradt

Pioneering guides to exceptional places

NOTES

Index

Page numbers in **bold** indicate main entries; those in *italics* indicate maps.

*This designation is without prejudice to positions on status, and is in line with UNSCR 1244/1999 and the ICJ Opinion on the Kosovo declaration of independence.